MARION D. CUYJET AND HER JUDIMAR SCHOOL OF DANCE

Training Ballerinas in Black Philadelphia 1948-1971

Marion Cuyjet circa 1950

Photograph by Gaston DeVigne Studio, Philadelphia, Pa.

Reproduced through the courtesy of the Marion D. Cuyjet Private Collection

MARION D. CUYJET AND HER JUDIMAR SCHOOL OF DANCE

Training Ballerinas in Black Philadelphia 1948-1971

Melanye White Dixon

With a Foreword by
Lynette Young Overby

The Edwin Mellen Press
Lewiston•Queenston•Lampeter

Library of Congress Cataloging-in-Publication Data

Dixon, Melanye White.
Marion D. Cuyjet and her Judimar School of Dance : training ballerinas in Black Philadelphia 1948-1971 / Melanye White Dixon ; with a foreword by Lynette Young Overby.
p. cm.
Includes bibliographical references and index.
ISBN-13: 978-0-7734-1592-8 (hardcover)
ISBN-10: 0-7734-1592-0 (hardcover)
1. Cuyjet, Marion. 2. Dance teachers--United States--Biography. 3. African American dance teachers--Biography. 4. Judimar School of Dance. 5. Dance--Study and teaching--Pennsylvania--Philadelphia--History--20th century. 6. Ballet--Pennsylvania--Philadelphia--History--20th century. 7. African American dance--Pennsylvania--Philadelphia--History--20th century. 8. African Americans--Pennsylvania--Philadelphia--History--20th century. I. Title.
GV1785.C89D59 2011
792.8092--dc23
[B]

2011019396

hors série.

A CIP catalog record for this book is available from the British Library.

Front cover photo: Marion Cuyjet, circa 1950. Photograph by Gaston DeVigne Studio

The Edwin Mellen Press
Box 450
Lewiston, New York
USA 14092-0450

The Edwin Mellen Press
Box 67
Queenston, Ontario
CANADA L0S 1L0

The Edwin Mellen Press, Ltd.
Lampeter, Ceredigion, Wales
UNITED KINGDOM SA48 8LT

Printed in the United States of America

To my parents

Carl Eldridge White and Nellie Clark White

For their everlasting love and support

and in loving memory of

Joe Nash

CONTENTS

List of Illustrations

13. Joan Myers Brown publicity photograph, circa 1960.

14. Judimar Dance Company, circa 1950.

15. Marion Cuyjet's parents, Frances Henrietta Morgan Dunham and Alonzo Durham, circa 1930.

16. Joe Nash performing L'Afrique, at the Judimar School of Dance, circa 1953.

17. First Staff of the Judimar School of Dance, Marion Cuyjet, Franca Jimenez,Terez Nelson, John Hines, and Shirley Elsey, circa 1948, photograph by Gaston DeVigne Studio.

18. Delores Browne, Franca Jimenez, and Judy Cuyjet in a Judimar School of Dance recital, circa 1954, photograph by GiJi.

19. Bon Voyage party for Ernest Leigh Parham, circa 1954.

20. Judimar School of Dance first recital performance, circa 1948, photograph by Gaston DeVigne Studio.

21. Marion Cuyjet with first scholarship students Alice Mays (Hall) and Juanita Jones (Fagan), circa 1949.

22. Alice Mays and Juanita Jones performing in Carmen for a Judimar School of Dance recital, circa 1951, photograph by Wert S. Hooper.

23. John Jones performing in London, circa 1960, photograph by Anthony Crickmay.

24. Alice Mays, Delores Browne, and Juanita Jones performing in a Judimar School of Dance recital, circa 1953, photograph by John W. Mosley.

25. Judy Cuyjet as Cinderella in a Judimar School of Dance recital, circa 1950.

26. Joyce Graves in a Judimar School of Dance recital, circa 1955.

27. Judimar Dance Company performs ballet excerpts for television program, circa 1957.

28. Delores Browne performing in Carmen for the Dra Mu Opera Company, circa 1951.

29. Delores Browne as a member of the New York Negro Ballet Company, circa 1956.

30. Donna Lowe and Elmer "Skeets" Ball in a ballet class at the Judimar School of Dance, circa 1955.

31. Judimar School of Dance recital performance of Giselle with Donna Lowe and Judith Jamison, circa 1956.

32. Judimar School of Dance tap class, circa 1953.

33 Elmer "Skeets" Ball partners Donna Lowe for a Judimar School of Dance recital, circa 1957, photograph by E. Barton.

34. Judith (Judy) Marion Cuyjet preparing to perform for the Philadelphia Christmas Cotillion Ball, circa 1960.

35. Elmer "Skeets" Ball with Katherine Dunham as a member of the Katherine Dunham Dance Company, circa 1959.

36. Elmer "Skeets" Ball in a professional portrait, circa 1965.

37. China White, Yvonne Hall, and Brenda Garrett (Glassman), as members of Dance Theatre of Harlem, circa 1971.

38. China White performing in Louis Johnson's *Forces of Rhythm* with Dance Theatre of Harlem, circa 1972.

39. Marion Cuyjet teaching ballet for Philadanco (Philadelphia Dance Company), circa 1995.

40. Marion Cuyjet giving corrections to Philadanco dancers, circa 1995.

Foreword

I have known Melanye White Dixon for many years as a dedicated dance educator. I was also aware of her scholarship regarding African American dance educators in the Philadelphia area. However, until I was asked to write this Foreword, I was not aware of the cultural connections and legacy of Mrs. Marion Cuyjet. I discovered that I might be a small part of that legacy. As I read Cuyjet's resume, I noted that she taught dance at Delaware State College from 1958 to 1960. As a child growing up in Dover, Delaware, a dance teacher first exposed me to ballet from Delaware State College. The year was 1959 and we were fortunate to have an African American dance teacher come to our small community to teach ballet and prepare us for a performance. I do not recall a great deal about the dance, but recognized much later that during a time of limited opportunities for African Americans to study dance in Dover, Delaware, this experience provided special memories for each of the young dancers fortunate to be a part of this experience. I believe Marion Cuyjet was that teacher.

Building on her doctoral work, Dr. Dixon utilizes multiple sources of data to tell Marion Cuyjet's story. Through interviews, historical documentation, and other media including newspapers, programs, and film, we learn how a determined spirit can overcome adversity in terms of racial discrimination and personal limitations. We learn about the importance of family and friendships that provided a safe haven of support for the development of future dancers. The list of dancers and affiliated teachers she nurtured and supported is impressive and provides a critical link to our knowledge of the black dance lineage. The list includes, Tawny Turner, Philadelphia Civic Ballet; China White, Dance Theatre of Harlem, John Jones, Harkness Ballet; and her most famous student, Judith Jamison, dancer and artistic director for the world-renowned Alvin Ailey American Dance Theatre. And, her legacy continues as her students have mentored others in the tradition of the Cuyjet approach.

And what exactly was that approach? A statement in the final chapter describes it as follows: "Cuyjet's teaching approach stressed performance and academic knowledge of the theory, craft, and history of ballet. She knew that proficiency in these areas would distinguish students from the average dancer. According to former students who pursued professional careers, Cuyjet's teaching approach prepared them for a world in which African Americans had to be technically superior in order to achieve minimal success."

Cuyjet is one of those rare teachers/individuals who have made a difference in the life and culture of a city, a nation, and in many students of dance. In addition to the story of dance, the material in this book also provides an important record of the social, economic, and cultural life styles of African Americans during the 30s, 40s, 50s, and 60s in Philadelphia. This is a book to share with anyone interested in a significant moment in the history of Philadelphia, and for dancers who are interested in their heritage.

My brief encounter with Marion Cuyjet was the beginning of a journey in dance that I still travel. Through the pages of this enjoyable and well-researched book, Dr. Dixon allowed me to look back and consider all that I have learned from pioneers like Marion Cuyjet—lessons about the determination one needs to pursue a passion through difficulty and adversity and the manner in which one person can make a difference in the life of a community.

Lynnette Young Overby, Ph.D.
Professor of Theatre and Dance
University of Delaware
Dover, Delaware

Dr. Lynnette Young Overby serves as Faculty Director of Undergraduate Research and Experiential Learning and Professor of Theatre and Dance at the University of Delaware. Her publications have appeared in *The Journal of Mental*

Imagery, The Journal of Physical Education, Recreation, and Dance, and the *Journal of Human Movement Studies.* With co-authors, Beth Post and Diane Newman, she published the book, Interdisciplinary Learning through Dance: 101 Moventures. In 2000 she was named the National Dance Association Organization Scholar/Artist and in 2006 was named a Senior Outreach Fellow at Michigan State University.

Acknowledgements

I would like to acknowledge and thank the many people who have assisted in the completion of this study. Special gratitude to Marion D. Cuyjet for her inspiration and gracious cooperation; John Hines for information on his professional and personal relationship with Mrs. Cuyjet; Sydney Gibson King for willingness to share fond memories of her life in dance and partnership with Cuyjet; Carolyn Shuttlesworth, a scholar and dance enthusiast who introduced me to Cuyjet; Mrs. Cuyjet's loving and generous family, daughter Judy Cuyjet, son Stephen Cuyjet Jr. and granddaughter Kaersten Colvin Woodruff.

My sincere appreciation to all who granted interviews, Elmer Ball, Charles L. Blockson, Delores Browne Abelson, Joan Myers Brown, Cyrus Carter, Dr. Noel Cazenave, Gary D. Celain, John Cooper, Judy Cuyjet, Stephen Cuyjet Jr., Arthur Hall, William Dollar, Reginald Farrar, Shirley Franklin, Robert Garland, Vera Gunn, John Hines, Mr. and Mrs. Percy Holmes, Mattie Humphrey, Judith Jamison, Franca Jimenez, Dorothy Kapenstein, Beverly Kealch, Sydney G. King, Althea Leslie, Dr. Richard Long, Dr. Patricia Reid-Merritt, Myrna Amai Munchus Bullock, Ione Nash, Joe Nash, Gail Nelson, Jerri Packman, Malcom Poindexter Jr., Harrison Riddley Jr, Doris Roberts, Faye Snow, James Spady, Eazell Stephens, Tawny Turner, Donna Lowe Warren, Karen Warrington, Dr. Clark White, China White, and Elizabeth Wilder.

I am grateful to The Ohio State University College of Arts and Humanities, and the Department of Dance for in-kind services, a faculty research leave, and manuscript preparation funding. I extend special appreciation and thanks to Dr. John Roberts for his support and encouragement. Sincere thanks to colleagues Vickie Blaine, Karen Bell, Dr. Vera Maletic, Odette Blum, Lucy Venable, Dr. Angelika Gerbes, Dr. Sheila Marion, M. Rosalind Pierson, John Giffin, Victoria Uris, Dr. Beverly Moss, and Dr. Linda Callahan for their enduring camaraderie and support. Sincere thanks to Temple University colleagues Dr. Kariamu Welsh,

Tina Sloan-Green, Dr. Sonia Peterson-Lewis, Dr. Molefi Kete Asante, Dr. Brenda Dixon Gottschild, Dr. Edrie Ferdum, Dr. Sarah Hilsendager, Dr. Sonia Sanchez, and Ira Shapiro, for their support and advice.

Special thanks to dance artists and educators Barbara Blake, Tamara Brown, Trudy Cobb, Alexis del Sol, Karen Hubbard, Karen King Cavin, Bernadine Jennings, Ronald K. Brown, Mary Hinkson, Maurice Hines, Valerie Rochon, Leah Bass, Aneka McMullen, Michelle Zada Hall and G.D. Harris.

I express my sincere thanks to the following individuals and institutions for granting me permission to reprint photographs from their archives: Judy Cuyjet, custodian of the Marion D. Cuyjet Private Collection; China White, Private Collection; Alexis Wilson Stripling, estate executrix of the Billy Wilson Collection; The Charles L. Blockson Afro-American Collection, Temple University Libraries. I am indebted to Charles L. Blockson, curator emeritus, Diane Turner director of the Charles L. Blockson Afro-American Collection, librarian Aslaku Berhanu, library assistant Ida Wesley, and associate archivist Leslie Willis Lowry.

Thanks to the staff members of the *Philadelphia Tribune*, Free Library of Philadelphia, New York Public Library for the Performing Arts Library Jerome Robbins Dance Division, Schomburg Center for Research in Black Culture, Joe Nash Collection, Samuel Paley Library at Temple University, University of the Arts Albert M. Greenfield Library and Bobst Library at New York University.

I extend my appreciation to Rachel Reiss for assistance with manuscript preparation, Dr. Müge Galin for her meticulous attention to editing, Patricia Schultz, production editor, for her guidance, Lori Gandy for assistance with digital imaging, and to John Rupnow and Barbara J. Burt for their support. Sincere gratitude to Dr. Lynette Young Overby, Dr. Barbara Cohen-Stratyner, Curator of Exhibitions, The New York Public Library for the Performing Arts, Florence A. Cobb, professor emeritus, Mankato State University, and Dr. Beverly Barbara, professor emeritus, Florida A&M University for their time and thoughtful feedback on the manuscript.

I would like to express sincere appreciation to dear friends Gwendolyn J. Grant, and Dr. Arnetia Maasha, whose consistent words of encouragement and enthusiasm for this project kept me focused and inspired.

Thanks to my parents, Mr. and Mrs. Carl and Nellie White, whose civic engagement and educational contributions encouraged me to understand the importance of giving back to my community. Sincere gratitude to my husband Kevin and daughter Maya, for their patience, support, encouragement, and unconditional love.

Introduction

My aspirations to dance were supported as an undergraduate student at Spelman College by my dance mentors Diana Ramos (Eleo Pomare Dance Company), Shirley Rushing (Rod Rodgers Dance Company), and Hildegarde B. Tornow (Atlanta Ballet). I received ardent support for my scholarly interest in documenting the lives of African American women in concert dance from Professor Christine King Farris (sister of Dr. Martin Luther King Jr.). Receiving research guidance from Black dance historian Joe Nash and studying with former Katherine Dunham dancer Syvilla Fort during my graduate dance education studies at Teachers College, Columbia University, further bolstered my interest in dance history. These educational experiences provided the foundation that inspired me to pursue a career as an artist/educator/historian committed to teaching and writing about African American dancers and their impact on shaping American dance.

I began research on dance education in Black Philadelphia in 1982. My interest stems from my experiences as a young dancer in New York City during the early 1970s. Many of the most accomplished dancers on the scene were from Philadelphia's Black community, and those I most admired. When I began my doctoral research, I was able to turn my curiosity into a formal investigation about the training these dancers received. Who were the dance educators responsible for nurturing their talent? My preliminary investigation revealed the work of Marion Durham Cuyjet (1920–1996).

Writing this book, grounded in my dissertation research, has been a joy and an amazing journey. I grew up in the racially segregated South in Chattanooga,

Tennessee during the 1950s, where securing formal dance preparation for an African American child was rare. In part, this is why Cuyjet's story of nurturing young Black dancers during this time period of racial inequality is so noteworthy.

Cuyjet established the Judimar School in 1948 in order to provide opportunities in concert dance preparation and performance for African American youth in Philadelphia. Her initial vision was to produce America's first Black ballerina. Early in the development of Judimar, her vision expanded to offering dance as a means of social, educational, recreational, and cultural development.

Cuyjet's school was a prime conduit in promoting and developing dance education in Black Philadelphia. Several of her students have pursued performing careers with such dance companies as Alvin Ailey American Dance Theatre, Philadelphia Dance Company (Philadanco), Jerome Robbins Ballet USA, Harkness Ballet, Katherine Dunham Dance Company, Rod Rodgers Dance Company, Arthur Hall Afro-American Dance Ensemble, Pennsylvania Ballet, Philadelphia Grand Opera Company, and Dance Theatre of Harlem.

Cuyjet began her formal dance studies during the mid-1930s with Black Philadelphia socialite Essie Marie Dorsey. Dorsey established a dance studio in Philadelphia in 1926, and she is credited with initiating classical ballet training in Black Philadelphia. (Brown, 1977, p. 12) In 1946, Cuyjet and colleague Sydney King became partners and opened the Sydney-Marion School of Dance.

King was also trained by Dorsey, and their mission was to continue the work begun by their teacher. Their alliance lasted until 1948. That year they ended their partnership and established their own schools. King founded the Sydney School of Dance and Cuyjet, the Judimar School.

Many of Cuyjet's former students have pursued professional dance careers as teachers and performers. She is responsible for nurturing the talents of Judith Jamison, dancer and former artistic director of the Alvin Ailey American Dance Theatre and her most well-known student, Arthur Hall (Arthur Hall Afro-American Dance Ensemble), John Jones (Jerome Robbins' Ballet USA and Harkness Ballet), Elmer Ball (Katherine Dunham Dance Company), Donna

Lowe Warren (Philadelphia Grand Opera Company), Delores Browne Abelson (New York Negro Ballet Company), Tamara Guillebeaux (Rod Rodgers Dance Company), China White (Pennsylvania Ballet and Dance Theatre of Harlem), and Hollie Wright (Philadanco).

Cuyjet opened a dance school because there were limited opportunities for Black youth to study dance in Philadelphia. She emerged during a time when Blacks were excluded from the mainstream of Philadelphia's social, cultural, educational, economic, and political structure. The federal government's attempt to upgrade the status of Black workers during this post-war era outraged many white Philadelphians. This tension existed because jobs in the transit system and automobile industry were being made available to Blacks. Interracial hostility was a dominant issue. (Franklin, 1979, p. 159)

Black Philadelphians have traditionally formulated their own agenda for survival. The result has been the creation of a "Black Philadelphia," which has established organizations and institutions dedicated to meeting the needs of its community. The Black cultural arts institutions which evolved in the late 1940s (Philadelphia Concert Orchestra, Dra Mu Opera Company, Heritage House) were part of an effort to preserve and promote the traditions of African American culture. The Heritage House, a component of the Philadelphia Cotillion Society, was the leading cultural arts institution until the early 1970s. Eugene Wayman Jones, founder of Heritage House, showcased Cuyjet and King's dancers for the prestigious Annual Heritage House Christmas Cotillion.

Marion Cuyjet's story addresses issues of racial identity, social justice, and social change. The emphasis of her school was ballet, unique to Black dance studios nationwide. She sometimes passed for white to open doors of opportunity for her students and forged partnerships with selected mainstream dance educators in Philadelphia and New York City who, like her, were dedicated to the demise of cultural apartheid in the dance world. In the last few years, I have received several inquiries regarding my initial research on Marion Cuyjet. A May 6, 2007 *New York Times* article: "Where are all the Black Swans," by Gia Kourlas, addressed the dearth of Black ballerinas in prominent ballet companies. I believe this article has encouraged writers and scholars to consider new conversations about racial politics in dance, especially ballet. There is curiosity about the era in which Cuyjet nurtured dancers in Philadelphia between 1948 and 1971. The groundbreaking 1954 Supreme Court case of *Brown vs. the Board of Education* set the stage for social change and equal opportunities for Black Americans. Cuyjet caught the wave of the early years of the Civil Rights Movement and encouraged her students to never allow the color of their skin to limit their aspirations.

Cuyjet was a dominant figure in cultivating a positive and nurturing environment for dancers and dance educators in Black Philadelphia. It is necessary to consider her family background, the phases of her professional preparation, teaching career, and the historical development of her dance school in order to understand how and why she attained the status as a renowned ballet pedagogue and guiding force of dance education in Black Philadelphia.

I met Cuyjet September 1984 and it was as if she had been waiting for someone to document her career because her memorabilia was extremely organized and her recollections were clear and detailed. Cuyjet rendered oral history that spanned the late 1920s to the late 1980s and interviews were conducted from 1984 to 1986. Our first interview occurred in November 1984 and it included information that enabled me to locate several key contacts. Her personal accounts were corroborated by information retrieved from interviews with her family, colleagues, and former students. Where information appeared to be inconsistent with Cuyjet's own recollections, I made the choice of deleting such information. The taped interviews proved to be invaluable sources of information because there is a limited amount of documentation on Cuyjet's work. Her private collection of newspaper clippings, scrapbooks, recital bulletins, lesson plans, letters, and photographs supplemented the interviews.

The foundation of *Marion D. Cuyjet and Her Judimar School of Dance: Training Ballerinas in Black Philadelphia 1948–1971* is based on an oral history of Cuyjet's teaching career from 1948 to 1971. Chapter One initiates her journey by giving an overview of Cuyjet's family background, her elementary and secondary school years, the teacher with whom her dancing life began and the circumstances surrounding her transition from student to teacher. Chapter Two examines Cuyjet's teaching approach during her independent teaching career. It focuses on the developmental training and teaching experiences which shaped the principles of her fundamental teaching approach. Chapter Three provides a social, cultural, and historical frame of reference for the period in which Cuyjet's school, Judimar, emerged and developed. It presents an overview of the general state of Black Philadelphia, its cultural arts organizations and institutions, and the state of dance education with emphasis on acknowledged proponents. Chapter Four examines the historical development and organizational structure of the Judimar School of Dance. In addition, it presents brief portraits of four former Judimar students who continue to perpetuate the dance preparation they received with Marion Cuyjet. Chapter Five presents a summary, analysis, and postscript that provides information regarding Cuyjet's career after the Judimar era and updates on selected former colleagues, faculty, and students who are ramifications of her legacy.

The text of *Marion D. Cuyjet and Her Judimar School of Dance* is an historical and descriptive study of the teaching career of Marion Cuyjet as seen in its socio-cultural perspective. The primary period of inquiry spans two decades, 1950 to 1970. It provides primary information for dance professionals (dancers, educators, scholars, and historians), researchers in African American Studies and Women's Studies, and the general public. It will enable these populations to evaluate Cuyjet's contributions to a tradition of excellence in dance education in Black Philadelphia.

This book was written in honor of Cuyjet's visionary work. I hope that it will encourage subsequent research on dance education in urban American communities in addition to documenting recent strides that are being made to prepare African American dancers for careers in concert dance.

CHAPTER 1

Beginnings and Inspiration to Dance

Early Life

Marion D. Cuyjet was born Marion Helene Durham on July 29, 1920 in Philadelphia, Pennsylvania. Cuyjet's father, Alonzo Durham, moved to Philadelphia from Chelswold, Delaware in the early 1900s. He and his wife, Frances, were members of a small Cheswold community of mixed blood people (Native American, Spanish, and West African) known as Delaware Moors (Weslager, 1943). Alonzo Durham secured employment in Philadelphia and sent for his wife and eldest son.

Durham started out as a paper-hanger and eventually found a job as a Navy yard oiler-engineer. Frances Durham was a housewife. Cuyjet had two older brothers: Archie, the eldest, and Norris, seven years her senior. The family settled in the Point Breeze section of South Philadelphia on Wilder Street. During that time, the majority of Black Philadelphians lived in South Philadelphia (Ballard, 1984, p. 184).

Cuyjet became interested in dance as a child. Her mother took her to neighborhood dance recitals given by Essie Marie Potts (Dorsey's first married name). The depression severely affected the Durham family's financial stability. They could not afford dance classes for their daughter, so they encouraged her to become involved with music. Frances Durham came from a long line of musicians, and Cuyjet's father and oldest brother played violin. Cuyjet states: "We already had a piano and my brother's accompanist, Gilbert Martin, agreed to give me piano lessons. My training was excellent, but I was a lousy pianist" (personal communication, November 29, 1984).

Cuyjet's initial dance experiences were through participation in the Alma Polk Kiddie Revue which was a once-a-year event in Black Philadelphia. The performers were all children. Rehearsals were usually six weeks, and the shows were held at the Elks Club at 16th and Fitzwater in the Octavius V. Catto auditorium (M.D. Cuyjet, personal communication, November 29, 1984). Cuyjet performed in the Polk Revue for three consecutive years at ages 10, 11, and 12. She performed with the Nicholas Brothers in two of the revues. The Nicholas Brothers were renowned tap dancers who came to prominence in the 1940s. Fayard Nicholas was 14 at the time and he taught Cuyjet a solo song and dance routine for one of the shows (M.D. Cuyjet, personal communication, November 29, 1984).

Cuyjet was growing up during an era when Philadelphia's Black population grew rapidly in size. This phenomenon was known as the Great Migration. From 1917 to 1930, thousands of Blacks went from the South to the urban North in search of better employment opportunities (Ballard, 1984, p. 184). Most of the newcomers in the "Quaker City" settled in North Philadelphia. They were referred to as the "New Philadelphians." Blacks whose families originated in Philadelphia were known as the "Old Philadelphians." During the Great Migration a subtle friction existed between these two communities. The "Old Philadelphia" status was perceived as superior to the status of the newcomers (Ballard, 1984, p. 187). As in Black urban communities nationwide, a Yankee heritage was a measure of distinction.

The fusion of Southern and Northern cultures created a modern Black Philadelphia with a rich tradition in music, literature, and sports (Ballard, 1984, pp. 217–229). In addition, the church played a vital role in the social life of many Black Philadelphians. Cuyjet's family attended First African Baptist Church at 16th and Christian.

Cuyjet attended Landreth Elementary School (1926–1931) and Barratt Junior High School (1931–1934). Both schools were informally desegregated with predominately white populations. Barratt offered extracurricular dance activities through its physical education program and Virginia Lingenfelder was the director. Cuyjet auditioned for the ballet and tap clubs, but was not accepted. She later joined the folk dance club at the invitation of another physical education teacher at the school (M.D. Cuyjet, personal communication, November 29, 1984). Cuyjet related well to most of her schoolmates and teachers. She states that during her elementary school years a few Black classmates taunted her because she looked white and she remembers running home from school occasionally to avoid physical confrontation (M.D. Cuyjet, personal communication, November 29, 1984).

When Cuyjet entered South Philadelphia High School in 1934, she began to have an active social life. She participated in recreational and social activities sponsored by her church and the Belmont Young Women's Christian Association (M.D. Cuyjet, personal communication, November 29, 1984). Cuyjet's introduction to formal dance studies was in 1934 at the age of 14. She fondly remembers the event by giving the following account:

> Some friends of mine from Sunday school told me that Essie Marie Potts was to reopen her studio. She had remarried and she came back into business as Essie Marie Dorsey. All my friends had invitations to the opening except me. I asked to go with them. I did not let my mother know about it because she would not let me go if I did not have an invitation. Classes were 25 cents. I only had enough money for "car fare" home. My friend "Wheedie" [Edith] Daniels loaned me the money for class. When I got to the school Mrs. Dorsey invited me to join the class (personal communication, November 29, 1984).

Cuyjet's dancing life began with Essie Marie Dorsey, who was later to become her confidante and mentor.

Essie Marie Dorsey

Essie Marie Dorsey was born on June 11, 1893 in Goldsboro, North Carolina to Elias and Jenny Perry. Dorsey left North Carolina as a child to go to New York to study dance. She was reared by her mother's aunt and uncle and she also spent time in Baltimore with an uncle who was a physician (P. Holmes, personal communication, January 24, 1986).

Dorsey (1893–1967) began her formal dance studies in New York in the 1920s. During this time the Harlem Renaissance was gaining momentum. This movement, whose impact lasted through the 1930s, was led by African American visual artists, writers, scholars, historians, and social scientists. Their mission was to document the cultural and intellectual achievements of the African Americans and to strengthen the cultural aspirations and traditions of the Black community (Drimmer, 1972, p. 419). Dorsey was not directly involved with this movement, but its mission undoubtedly served to inspire her pursuit of concert dance, an arena considered "off limits" to Black dancers during that era.

Dorsey studied modern dance with Ruth St. Denis and Ted Shawn and tap at the Billy Pierce dance studio in New York City. She took private ballet classes with Michel Fokine and Mikhail Mordkin (pioneers in the development of American ballet), and received extensive training in Spanish dancing from Angel Cansino, son of Andalusian dance master Antonio Cansino (E.M. Dorsey, Private Collection). Dorsey passed for white in order to take group class at the Cansino studio. Her light, olive complexion gave the appearance of a person of Spanish descent. She wore a scarf-like head wrap to disguise her hair texture. Without it, her racial identity could be detected (P. Holmes, personal communication, January 24, 1986). African Americans were not granted admission to most professional New York dance studios before 1940 unless they passed for white or could afford private lessons (J. Nash, personal communication, August 16, 1985).

Dorsey's forte was Spanish dance. She was a featured dancer with Mikhail Mordkin's first American-based ballet company in the mid-1920s and performed exclusively in classical Spanish pieces. Although she and Mordkin were friends, she was not invited to be an understudy or perform in any of the company's classical ballet works. She was considered a "special" rather than a regular member of the Mordkin company (E. M. Dorsey, private collection). Her ultimate goal was a career in ballet, but the only arenas open to Black dancers during that era were nightclubs, vaudeville, and Broadway.

Dorsey decided to direct her performance energy toward a teaching career. Her areas of specialization were Spanish dance and classical ballet. She lived in Atlantic City, New Jersey, and Baltimore, Maryland before moving to Philadelphia. Perhaps Dorsey chose to relocate to Philadelphia because of its rich ballet tradition: during the post-revolutionary war era, Philadelphia became the center of academic ballet; in the 1800s, the Paul Hazzard Studio produced renowned American dancers Augusta Maywood and Mary Ann Lee; in the 1930s, Catherine Littlefield formed in this city the first classical ballet company composed of American dancers (Maynard, 1982, pp. 20–21).

Dorsey married Philadelphian H. LaBarr Potts in 1923, and in 1926 she opened her first Philadelphia dance studio in her home at 1208 South 48th Street (E.M. Dorsey, Private Collection). In the mid-1920s, Dorsey moved her studio to 525 South Broad Street and in the late 1930s, to 711 South Broad Street. She operated a small school in New York City in 1929 and one in Baltimore, Maryland in 1932. Dorsey occasionally rented out her Philadelphia studios as rehearsal space to dance companies on tour. Ballet Caravan, a development of the American Ballet Company, directed by Lincoln Kirstein, frequented Dorsey's studio (Brown, 1977, p. 12).

Dorsey's Philadelphia studio offered courses in ballet, tap, acrobatics, and ballroom dance. She taught ballet, acrobatics, and ballroom dance, and Blacky Johnson taught tap (J. Hines, personal communication, July 24, 1985). Thomas Cannon, a well-known Philadelphia ballet teacher who operated his own school and was principal dancer with the Littlefield Ballet Company, also taught ballet (S. King, personal communication, February 25, 1985). Cannon and Dorsey were close friends and occasionally he invited some of Dorsey's students to study at his school. According to Cuyjet, Cannon was the only white dance teacher during that era who taught Black students. He held separate classes for them because he feared that if he desegregated classes at his school, he would lose his clientele (M.D. Cuyjet, personal communication, November 29, 1984).

Most of Dorsey's students were female and ranged in age from 3 to 12 (E.M. Dorsey, Private Collection). When she opened her school, she recruited students by going door to door in her immediate neighborhood. Many of the parents she talked with were skeptical because they strongly believed that dance was not a proper leisure activity for children. Their reservations could probably be attributed to vestiges of Victorian and Protestant beliefs that dance was unwholesome, if not unholy (S.G. King, personal communication, February 25, 1985). Dorsey started her school with five students: Sydney Gibson (King), Jean Hedgepatch (Lewis), Ruth Hampton, Susie Payton, and Gertrude Hopson (Brown, 1977, p. 12). As her school enrollment increased, she sent out formal printed invitations and announcements. In the early 1930s, Dorsey began to attract child entertainers who performed on the "Colored Kiddie Hour," a popular show on WPEN, a local Philadelphia radio station (R. Fontell, Private Collection).

Dorsey's lavish recitals became popular events in Black Philadelphia and they usually ran three consecutive nights. Her first Philadelphia recital was on June 16, 1927 at the New Century Drawing Room, 214 South 12th Street (E.M. Dorsey, Private Collection). Additional performance outlets included the National Association for the Advancement of Colored People fund raisers, church teas, recreation centers and Elks club programs. The majority of these performances were presented in Black Central City Philadelphia (M.D. Cuyjet, personal communication, November 29, 1984).

Dorsey continued to study ballet when she moved to Philadelphia. She studied privately with Thomas Cannon who used the Cecchetti method of teaching ballet. She also studied with dancer-choreographer William Dollar, whom she met through the Mordkin Ballet. When the company temporarily disbanded due to lack of funds in the late 1920s, Dorsey offered Dollar accommodations in her home until he secured another dance position (M.D. Cuyjet, personal communication, September 11, 1985). Dollar reciprocated in kind: "I gave Essie ballet class each morning when I lived with her" (W. Dollar, personal communication, February 16, 1986).

Besides her career as a dance teacher, Dorsey, described as dynamic and glamorous by former student Joan Myers Brown, established a reputation as a Black socialite and a prominent community organizer (see Plate 2). She was the founder of the Germantown Civic League, a charter member of the Philadelphia Grande Opera Company, and the Philadelphia Cotillion Society. She wrote a social graces column for the *Philadelphia Independent*, an African American publication, and directed the Dra Ma Opera Company's Dance Department (Brown, 1977 p. 12).

Dorsey closed her first school in 1933. She divorced her first husband, H. LaBarr Potts, and married Carroll Dorsey, a well-known Philadelphia caterer. She reopened her school in 1934 under the name Essie Marie Dorsey. On October 1, 1939, Dorsey initiated a cultural arts symposium series. The monthly programs showcased dancers, musicians, singers, and orators. Each program featured a different performer. The purpose of the symposium series was "to develop an appreciation of all types of art and develop and promote our aspiring local artists" (E.M. Dorsey, Private Collection).

Her former students remember Dorsey as a taskmaster who believed in "old fashioned" etiquette. Cuyjet states: "Students were required to curtsy or bow on entering the building, entering class, leaving class, and leaving the building" (personal communication, November 29, 1984). Her fundamental teaching approach revolved around positive reinforcement, the hands-on method of touching students to correct body placement, and mini dance history lectures focusing on inspirational scenarios of famous dancers. Cuyjet states:

> Once Dorsey brought in an article on Patricia Bowman, an American dancer. She was a chorus girl who began to study ballet in her late

> twenties and became a ballerina. Mrs. Dorsey marveled at the fact that a person who had no training as a child in any form of dance could achieve such an accomplishment. (personal communication, September 11, 1985)

Dorsey was firm, but kind, and outside of dance classes, she took a personal interest in many of her students. Realizing Cuyjet could not afford regular classes, Dorsey awarded her a full scholarship. According to Cuyjet, a close bond developed between the two of them. Cuyjet states: "She was like an aunt to me" (personal communication, September 11, 1985). In the mid-1930s, Dorsey arranged for Cuyjet to receive private lessons with Thomas Cannon and to study with the Littlefield Ballet Company and School, the precursor to the Pennsylvania Ballet.

Cuyjet states:

> Dorsey was very close to the directors of the school, yet they never permitted her to take classes there. She passed me off [as white] so I could enroll in the school. She paid for my tuition; however, I had to go alone to register for school. I studied and danced with the company while I was at Essie Marie's school. I was sixteen at the time. I did not perform on pointe. I was a part of the ensemble [corps]. The only person who knew I was Black was Thomas Cannon. Essie Marie had to confide in someone at that school. She chose him [Cannon] because they were friends. I remember performing at Wanamakers department store in the Greek auditorium. In those days, Wanamakers was open on Wednesday and Friday nights. We had two performances at the store, one on each night. I was never used for two performances because we did not have the same ballet twice in one week. My time there [at the school] was very short lived. It was quite an experience to be in a corps de ballet. My name was not Marion Durham. I used another name. I was discovered by my friends who attended Sunday school with me at the First African Baptist Church. I guess one of them saw me performing there. I never really knew how it happened. Anyway, they came as a group to one of the performances and came backstage to see me afterwards. For a group of colored girls to come back stage to ask to see one of the dancers was definitely unusual in those days. They [the directors of the school] figured it out [that I was passing for white] right away. Before they could tell me, Thomas Cannon told Essie to tell me not to come back. After that Essie had Cannon teach me privately. (personal communication, November 29, 1984)

Dorsey laid the groundwork for the acceptance of concert dance and formal dance studies in Black Philadelphia. In addition to Cuyjet, she nurtured John Hines, Sydney King, and Ann Bernadino Hughes, second-generation dance educators who had an immense impact on dance education in Black Philadelphia.

Student to Teacher

Sydney Gibson was Dorsey's leading dancer when Cuyjet came to the school. Cuyjet, 14, and Gibson, 13, became friends and dance school companions. During class breaks they used the studio to take turns coaching each other. They excelled in all their dance classes, and Dorsey promoted them, along with another friend, Ann Bernadino, to student-teacher status. Cuyjet, Gibson, and Bernadino composed Dorsey's first student-teaching team. Cuyjet and Gibson were responsible for children's ballet and Bernadino, for tap dance.

Cuyjet and Gibson taught under close supervision. Dorsey observed all their classes and they were never permitted to teach class in her absence. Cuyjet states:

> She would critique us after each class. She watched us carefully with the children's foot positions. We had a tendency to force them into fifth position. She stressed the importance of using first and second foot positions and natural walks and runs in beginning children's classes. She constantly reminded us about the teacher/pupil relationship. She said there was to be no mothering, to be professional, but not distant. My problem was that I was too stern. Sydney was always giggling. (personal communication, September 11, 1985)

Dorsey's encouragement and Cuyjet's initial teaching experiences enhanced her interest in dance education. Dorsey's mentoring enabled Cuyjet to begin formulating her teaching approach. Cuyjet comments on Dorsey's influence:

> I learned to teach from the positive angle. She told me that I must look at each child as a promising ballerina and teach that child in that manner, have her work for perfection. Approach her as though she is the

> only one in class. Treat each child special. Find something that she did better than before, each class. I've never forgotten this. (personal communication, September 11, 1985)

During Cuyjet's student teaching years, she emulated Dorsey's teaching style. She copied her verbal dynamics and began to use Cecchetti ballet technique.

Cuyjet married Billy Hendrix at age 18 and discontinued her dance studies. She had been married a little over six months when Dorsey asked her to come back to the school to replace her secretary. Cuyjet became an assistant teacher and resumed taking classes. Dorsey taught Cuyjet ballroom dance. "I was responsible for teaching all of the private day-time ballroom classes. I loathed it. Once, Mrs. Dorsey caught me on my knees trying to move a client's feet in the correct positions" (personal communication, September 11, 1985).

Cuyjet's first child, Judy, was born in 1940. Her marriage dissolved in 1941 and at age 21, she divorced her first husband. She left Dorsey's school and found employment in Chester, Pennsylvania at Sun Ship, a ship-building company. Cuyjet worked in the time-keeping department. While working there, she assisted in the production of an employee variety musical and dance show (M.D. Cuyjet, personal communication, September 25, 1985). In 1944, at age 24 Cuyjet married Stephen Cuyjet, a serviceman in the United States Army (see Plate 3). A year later there was the birth of her first son, Stephen, Jr. Stephen Cuyjet left the service and the family settled in the Germantown section of Philadelphia on Upsal Street. Stephen Cuyjet was employed as a postal clerk and industrial arts teacher. Cuyjet left Sun Ship to become a full-time wife and mother.

Cuyjet had the desire to renew her involvement with dance. Thomas Cannon suggested that she study folk dance with Nancy Lynch, an instructor at Temple University at the time. Cuyjet states: "I took folk dance to get back into the swing of things" (personal communication, September 25, 1985). Cuyjet went to Lynch for private folk dance classes and fundamentals of children's dance. She felt that she was in no position to pursue a career as a dancer. Her first priority was her family and she realized that she did not have the stamina for the rigorous life of a performer. Cuyjet chose to pursue a teaching career instead. Stephen Cuyjet was aware of his wife's desire to teach and encouraged her to establish a school (M.D. Cuyjet, personal communication, July 18, 1985).

She began teaching in her home in 1945. Her daughter suffered with rheumatic fever and doctors suggested dance as physical therapy for her heart condition. She decided to teach Judy at home. In order that her daughter would not have to take class alone, she invited Judy's favorite playmates to join the class at no charge. Cuyjet transformed their living room into a dance studio. She asked a neighborhood plumber to construct ballet barres out of pipes. She states: "We had very little furniture in the living room so we had plenty of space" (personal communication, July 18, 1985). Judy displayed an aptitude for dance and her heart condition improved. Cuyjet secured additional classes for Judy with Cannon, who was teaching at a private dance studio in Maplewood Mall in Germantown (M.D. Cuyjet, personal communication, July 18, 1985).

Cuyjet called Sydney Gibson King the summer of 1946 with the idea of establishing a dance school. At that time she was 26 and King was 25. It had been seven years since they had corresponded, and King had married in the interim. King was apprehensive about the idea, but Cuyjet finally convinced her and the Sydney-Marion School of Dance opened in the Fall of 1946 (M.D. Cuyjet, personal communication, November 29, 1984). Cuyjet had just begun private ballet lessons with Cannon, and she persuaded King to join the class.

Essie Marie Dorsey closed her studio during World War II to take up defense work. She turned her advanced students over to Cannon, and he trained these students as the ballet unit for the Dra Mu Opera Company. He taught them at his school in the special classes for Black students that were held on Monday nights (M.D. Cuyjet, personal communication, November 29, 1984). Dorsey planned to reopen her school in 1946, but changed her mind when she learned that Cuyjet and King planned to open a school. She offered them her former studio at 711 South Broad Street, and Dorsey assisted Cuyjet and King in establishing their school. "Mrs. Dorsey called us her hobby" (M.D. Cuyjet, personal communication, September 25, 1985). She handled most of their public relations work and was influential in placing articles about their school in the Black press (M.D. Cuyjet, personal communication, September 25, 1985) (see Plate 4).

Cuyjet discussed her plans to open a dance school with Cannon. His response was: "Your people need a school. The sooner the better" (M.D. Cuyjet, personal communication, November 29, 1984). He was extremely supportive of the idea and decided to include dance theory in the private sessions he conducted with her. Cuyjet recounts those sessions:

> Cannon explained the rationale for the order of a ballet class and coached me in the correct spelling and pronunciation of ballet terminology. He insisted that I take notes. He often explained the "why" of execution and I learned my first techniques in observing students in a dance class. He taught me how to prepare bookkeeping records for our school and I learned how to make a tutu, and the basics of ballet. costume construction (personal communication, September 25, 1985)

Throughout Cuyjet's career Cannon remained an ardent supporter. He loaned her costumes, props, and attended several of her school's recitals. Cuyjet studied with Cannon until 1951. She states: "I became involved with the New York dance teachers. It was a gradual breaking away" (personal communication, September 25, 1985).

During Cuyjet and King's partnership their roles were clear-cut. King was the main ballet instructor and Cuyjet handled most of the managerial and business matters. Cuyjet comments: "The feeling which prevailed during our years in business was that Sydney was the dancer and I the business woman" (personal communication, July 18, 1985). King taught most of the ballet and acrobatic classes and Cuyjet taught folk dance, the preschool group and beginner adult ballet classes. Mary Sherill, a student teacher, taught tap.

The school operated during the winter and spring seasons. Classes were held two afternoons a week and all day on Saturdays. In three months the enrollment increased and they added more days for a full-time schedule. Each work day concluded at 7:30 p.m.

John Hines, a mutual friend from Dorsey's school, began teaching Dunham Technique at the studio in 1946. Hines, recently discharged from the United States Army, had been studying dance at the Dunham School in New York City with the assistance of a grant under the G.I. Bill. Katherine Dunham, dancer, choreographer, and anthropologist, established the Dunham School of Dance in 1945. One of her principal motivations in establishing the school was to provide an outlet whereby African American dancers could receive comprehensive dance preparation (White-Dixon, 1984, p. 2).

Hines introduced Cuyjet and King to the Dunham Technique. Cuyjet fondly remembers the events of her first experience:

> Hines came to our studio one night with a tambour under one arm. Neither of us had seen him in quite some time. We were just getting ready to leave. He gave us a half hour class. We were so excited. (personal communication, July 18, 1985)

Hines insisted that Cuyjet and King come to New York to study at the Dunham School. They studied once a week during the 1947 summer session. Cuyjet went alone for the 1948 summer session. She made lodging arrangements at the Tatum House Young Women's Christian Association on 38th and Lexington Avenue. Cuyjet attended class four times a week during the 1948 session. Stephen Cuyjet drove her to New York each week (M.D. Cuyjet, personal communication, July 18, 1985).

Cuyjet studied Dunham Technique, Primitive Rhythms and Afro-Caribbean dance forms at the Dunham School (see Plate 5). Her teachers were Tommy Gomez, Talley Beatty, and Walter Nicks, all Dunham Company members. Nicks was Cuyjet's favorite teacher. She states: "He was very thorough" (personal communication, September 25, 1985).

Cuyjet enjoyed studying at the Dunham School despite a strained relationship with the registrar, Verne Van Beynum. She states:

> The registrar gave Sydney and I a hard time. She interviewed us in her office. She feared that we were going to take exact Dunham lessons back to Philadelphia and teach them. She must have thought we were. better than we were. (personal communication, September 25, 1985)

The Dunham School administrators were suspicious of Cuyjet and King. Cuyjet states: "They watched us very carefully" (personal communication, September 25, 1985). They finally approached Cuyjet and King with a proposition to place a Dunham teacher in their Philadelphia studio. The Sydney-Marion School of Dance consented to accept a Dunham teacher. The Dunham residency did not increase their enrollment substantially, but it attracted an adult population, Black and white, with prior dance experience. Their first New York based Dunham instructor was Syvilla Fort, ballet mistress and dancer with the Dunham Company and supervisor of the Dunham School's dance department. Cuyjet and King publicized Fort's classes extensively (see Plate 6). She taught once a week and an average class size was 25 to 30 students (M.D. Cuyjet, personal communication, September 25, 1985).

During Fort's residency (1947–1948), the Dunham School sent a Dunham Company presentation to Philadelphia. The concert was a cabaret-style production which consisted of ballet, modern, and Afro-Caribbean dance pieces. The lead male dancer was Walter Nicks (M.D. Cuyjet, personal communication, September 25, 1985).

Fort left the Sydney-Marion School of Dance because of her demanding administrative, teaching, and performing schedule. The Dunham School sent Eleanor Chapin, a white woman, to replace her. Chapin moved to Philadelphia. Cuyjet and King were not pleased with the new teacher and Fort's replacement stayed only a short time. Cuyjet suspects that the Dunham School had hopes of developing a Philadelphia branch, but it never materialized (M.D. Cuyjet, personal communication, July 18, 1985).

The Sydney-Marion School of Dance remained in existence two years, from 1946 to 1948. Cuyjet and King encountered management differences and decided to dissolve their partnership. Although short lived, this venture enabled both women to establish themselves as emerging dance educators in Black Philadelphia. King remained at the studio at 711 Broad Street and founded the Sydney School of Dance and Cuyjet opened the Judimar School of Dance in center city Philadelphia in 1948 (M.D. Cuyjet, personal communication, November 29, 1984).

By establishing the Judimar School of Dance, Cuyjet embarked on a journey in which she would discover herself as an accomplished teacher, artist, and visionary. The roots of her teaching style, whose groundwork had been laid by her first teacher, Essie Marie Dorsey, developed into a legacy which produced major artists in concert and theater dance in the ensuing decades. This pedagogical approach will be examined in the following chapter.

CHAPTER 2

Teaching Approach

Developmental Experience

During the initial stages of her independent teaching career, Cuyjet realized that she needed additional dance preparation. Thomas Cannon advised Cuyjet not to be discouraged by her lack of advanced teaching skills. He told her: "Just as long as you are half a page ahead of your students, you'll be okay" (M.D. Cuyjet, personal communication, November 29, 1984). Cuyjet accepted the challenge and persistently sought opportunities to increase her teaching proficiency in ballet by taking classes and reading extensively on ballet pedagogy. She studied ballet throughout the Judimar era and was determined to become a leading ballet pedagogue. John Hines, Cuyjet's friend and colleague, refers to Cuyjet as a self-made balletomane (J. Hines, personal communication, July 24, 1985). The dance preparation and teaching experiences Cuyjet received after she and King dissolved their partnership had an immense impact on her teaching approach.

Teacher Preparation

In 1948, the year Cuyjet founded the Judimar School of Dance, she began studying at the William Sena Ballet School located on 20th and Chestnut Streets. Sena was a former member of the resident ballet company at La Scala in Milan, Italy. Cuyjet studied with him sporadically until 1950 (M.D. Cuyjet, personal communication). Cuyjet remembers Sena as a genteel and gracious person. She states that the students called him "Papa Sena." He used a wooden rod as a teaching prop during class. He pounded it on the floor to keep time with the music, as a barre to assist students who encountered balance problems, and to lean on while standing. Cuyjet was impressed with Sena's methods. According to her, the porte de bras combinations were lovely and Sena's work was rounded and flowing (M.D. Cuyjet, personal communication, September 25, 1985).

Cuyjet and Sena became friends. He encouraged her to join the National Association of Dance and Affiliated Artists (NADAA) and occasionally invited her to teach seminars and workshops for the NADAA conventions in Philadelphia. This organization was composed of dance teachers, dancers, and musicians associated with community and private dance studios. The primary focus was promoting quality dance instruction and production.

John Hines also played a key role in Cuyjet's professional development. He coached her for independent solo performances, recommended New York-based dance teachers, and introduced her to the most recent trends in teaching (see Plate 7). Cuyjet states that Hines led her into several theories of teaching and he mesmerized her with lengthy discussions on innovative teaching approaches which he gleaned from his New York teachers. Hines encouraged Cuyjet to use this pedagogical information in her classes (personal communication, November 29, 1984).

In 1950, Hines suggested that Cuyjet study in New York City again. This time he recommended Vladimir Dokoudowsky, a teacher at Ballet Arts, located at Carnegie Hall. Dokoudowsky was a ballet dancer and teacher who performed with the Mordkin Ballet, Ballet Theatre, Ballet Russe de Monte Carlo, and the original Ballet Russes in the late 1930s (Cohen-Stratyner, 1982, p. 264). Cuyjet enrolled in Dokoudowsky's ballet and character class. His teaching approach was grounded in Russian classical ballet technique. Cuyjet comments on Dokoudowsky's appearance and demeanor in class by stating: "He was a chain smoker and wore tattered jazz shoes to class. He watched his class like a hawk" (personal communication, September 25, 1985). Cuyjet borrowed a few aspects of Dokoudowsky's teaching method such as using voice cues to indicate the dynamics for a particular movement (M.D. Cuyjet, personal communication, September 25, 1985).

The attractive feature of studying in New York was that the dance schools were integrated, and this enabled her to take her students. (Professional New York dance studios began to adopt a desegregation policy after the late 1940s. This was a major shift from the Dorsey era.) Cuyjet studied at Ballet Arts during the summer and winter sessions from 1950 to 1957. During the summer she brought her advanced students. Delores Browne, Cuyjet's star pupil in the early 1950s, took Dokoudowsky's class. According to Cuyjet, he was impressed by the young student's ballet technique.

Cuyjet eventually studied with additional teachers at Ballet Arts: Vera Nemtchinova, Valentina Pereyaslavec, and Lisan Kay. Nemtchinova was a Russian ballet dancer who performed with Diaghilev's Ballet Russes in the 1920s and the Ballet Russe de Monte Carlo in the 1930s (Cohen-Stratyner, 1982, p. 905). She was not performing at the time Cuyjet studied with her, yet she was physically capable of executing certain adagio movement combinations during the barre phase of class. Cuyjet comments on Nemtchinova's presence in class: "She smoked in class and taught sitting down. She taught from her performance memory. She used a demonstrator and hardly gave any corrections in class" (personal communication, September 25, 1985). It was evident that Nemtchinova was more performer than teacher, but Cuyjet was motivated by her total involvement with the performance aspect of classical ballet.

Cuyjet observed Valentina Pereyaslavec's class before joining it. Pereyaslavec was a Ukrainian dancer and teacher, and during her career she performed with the Kharkiv Ballet and the Sverdlovsk Opera Ballet (Wilson, 1974, p. 383). Several of Cuyjet's students studied with Pereyaslavec. Cuyjet states: "She was around forty years old; she was square in physique. She wore Cuban heeled tap shoes for class. She would tap her heel on a wooden box to beat out the meter of the music" (personal communication, September 25, 1985).

According to Cuyjet, Pereyaslavec seemed to meditate briefly before presenting each movement combination. She displayed a kind of spiritual connectedness with the movement (M.D. Cuyjet, personal communication, September 25, 1985).

Lisan Kay was an American-trained ballet dancer who toured Europe and America as an independent artist in the 1930s and 1940s (Cohen-Stratyner, 1982, p. 480). Kay taught adult ballet classes at Ballet Arts and Cuyjet took her evening beginning ballet classes. Kay suggested that Cuyjet study children's ballet pedagogy with her at the Ballet Repertory School in New York City. Cuyjet studied pedagogy with Kay during the winter of 1950 for about eight weeks. Classes were held during the week from nine in the morning to six in the evening. Cuyjet attended a few Saturday classes for supervised practice-teaching sessions. The curriculum included the opportunity for student teaching in a controlled environment and also covered methods and materials for teaching ballet and readings on child development with an emphasis on a child's motor development. Kay stressed the importance of teaching children the eight basic locomotor movements: runs, walks, gallops, hops, leaps, slides, skips, and jumps. Cuyjet began to formulate her approach to teaching ballet to children based on her experience in Kay's class at Ballet Repertory (M.D. Cuyjet, personal communication, October 2, 1985).

During the period Cuyjet studied at Ballet Arts, she also studied with George Chaffee. Chaffee danced with the Mordkin Ballet and the Fokine Ballet in the late 1930s, but was best known as a teacher and iconographer (Cohen-Stratyner, 1982, p. 165). After class at Ballet Arts, Cuyjet and her students would walk around the corner to Chaffee's studio on 58th Street. Chaffee held morning and evening classes and on holidays he added additional classes so that Cuyjet's students could receive intensive training. Cuyjet comments on his teaching method by stating: "Chaffee claimed he was from the French School of ballet training [but] he incorporated a great deal of Cecchetti and Russian technique. For our benefit, he would announce the times when he was on the Russian tangent" (personal communication, October 2, 1985).

Chaffee occasionally sat on a bench to teach during the barre, and he always stood for adagio combinations. He used a wooden rod as a teaching prop. He pounded it on the floor when angry, but most often he used it to assist students in maintaining their balance during the adagio center floor combinations. Cuyjet says that Chaffee's disposition in class was pleasant. "He was very charming, and personable, never aloof. He moved around during the pliés and developpés. He would align a shoulder, an elbow, turn a chin, or level it" (personal communication, October 2, 1985).

Chaffee's class procedure was in the traditional ballet mode. He began with barre work, proceeded to an adagio combination, and then he separated the class into female and male groups. The women executed allegro and pointe work and the men performed high jumps, leaps, and turns in the air. The class concluded with across the floor combinations. Cuyjet began to understand the importance of separating male and female virtuoso work through her experiences in his classes. He had sets of favorite dance combinations which he would repeat through the years. Many of these became Cuyjet's favorites and she recorded them on three-by-five cards. Cuyjet made variations on these combinations for her classes at Judimar. Chaffee became her mentor. She states: "He made an indelible impression on me. He sort of replaced Essie Marie Dorsey. I believe Chaffee took an interest in me because he was impressed that I came with my students" (personal communication, October 2, 1985). Cuyjet studied with Chaffee until 1968. That year she had to discontinue dancing because of a spinal operation. When she resumed teaching, she visited Chaffee's studio only to observe classes.

In 1956, Chaffee introduced Cuyjet to jazz dance. He referred to it as American jazz. One day after class he said: "I want you to watch this [jazz dance] carefully, this is the coming thing" (M.D. Cuyjet, personal communication, October 2, 1985). Chaffee surprised Cuyjet with a visit to the Matt Mattox studio on 54th Street and Broadway. After observing class first, she enrolled at the studio. Mattox was a jazz dancer who danced for film, musical theatre, and television in the 1950s and 1960s (Cohen-Stratyner, 1982, p. 596). Cuyjet describes his jazz dance style as angular and his demeanor in class as calm and low keyed. As far as feedback, "He stayed in the middle of the road: no accolades, no criticism" (personal communication, October 2, 1985). He demonstrated for class, but never danced with his students. He played a tambour and would cluck his tongue for accompaniment. There was never live musical accompaniment. Cuyjet studied with him until 1959.

Cuyjet discovered that the June Taylor School of Dance was in the same building as the Mattox studio. She studied jazz dance and the Tiller Line System at the Taylor School. Cuyjet comments on the Tiller System of teaching precision-line chorus dancing: "Each dance skill had a number, and class was taken in four inch heels. June Taylor's sister, Marilyn, taught the Tiller System" (personal communication, October 2, 1985). Cuyjet studied at the Taylor studio until 1964.

Cuyjet studied several jazz dance styles and specialized in the Luigi technique. She was introduced to the Luigi School by Llewellyn Wimberly, a Philadelphian who was studying at the Julliard School in the late 1950s. Cuyjet describes her relationship with Wimberly: "Llewellyn was younger than I, but took an interest in me because he liked what I was doing [at Judimar]. He was an excellent dancer and teacher" (personal communication, October 2, 1985). Wimberly persuaded Cuyjet to take some time off from her teaching schedule to study with Luigi. Cuyjet began studying with Luigi in 1957. His studio was located in the Jack Stanley Building on Eighth Avenue in the theater district of New York City. Luigi, a jazz dance choreographer and teacher, began his career in the early 1950s. He was involved in an auto accident which left him paralyzed on the right side of his body. His jazz dance technique evolved from the rehabilitation regime that he designed for himself. He developed a systematic series of exercises using the total body in each movement phrase (Kraines and Kan, 1983, p. 14).

Cuyjet characterized his style as both round and angular. "Body contractions were executed on oblique lines with torso twist, with the pelvis remaining centered" (M.D. Cuyjet, personal communication, October 2, 1985). Cuyjet describes a Luigi class:

> He began with exercises on the floor, then moved to the center floor exercises standing, and finished with one chorus length combination. There were no typical body part combinations. All movements were combined. The advanced class had a different dance combination each day. We never did across the floor movement. The class never stopped. He walked around during class. You were never criticized. A pianist and a drummer provided musical accompaniment. (personal communication, October 2, 1985)

There were usually about fifty people in a class. The population included dance students, teachers, and professional dancers. Luigi always acknowledged, by name, the "gypsies" (Broadway dancers) in attendance.

Cuyjet occasionally brought students from Judimar to study at Luigi's studio. She studied with Luigi from 1957 to 1968 during the summer and winter sessions. They became personal friends and he endorsed her as a Philadelphia-based Luigi specialist (M.D. Cuyjet, personal communication, October 2, 1985).

In 1965, Cuyjet began to study in Philadelphia with dancer-choreographer-teacher Joan Kerr, who was an exponent of Horton Technique and founded Philadelphia's first integrated modern dance company in 1964. (Kerr died in 1983 and her company disbanded shortly after her death.) In the same period, some of Cuyjet's advanced dancers studied modern dance with Kerr. Cuyjet and Kerr held mutual respect for each other's work, and she states that they had similar teaching temperaments. Both were firm taskmasters with stern teaching dispositions (personal communication, October 2, 1985).

Cuyjet went to Kerr for rehabilitation purposes. In 1961, she incurred a foot injury due to a fall while teaching class, which caused the amputation of a toe on her right foot. Consequently, she began to use her left leg as the support leg while teaching. As a result, the musculature supporting her right knee weakened. Her doctor recommended dance therapy in a different dance medium (personal communication, October 2, 1985).

Cuyjet chose Kerr because of her reputation as a demanding teacher. She studied with Kerr three times a week for nine months during 1965. Cuyjet states: "Kerr rehabilitated that knee. She told me that having me in class was like a piece of sunshine in her life" (personal communication, October 2, 1985). Kerr and Cuyjet cultivated a lasting friendship. In March (11–13), 1965, Cuyjet performed as a choral reader with Kerr's dance company in a performance of *Childermas*. In December 1965, Cuyjet invited Kerr to teach a Horton Technique class for Judimar's holiday seminar (G. Celain, Private Collection). Cuyjet's contact with Kerr influenced her jazz dance teaching style and she began to integrate fundamental elements of Horton Technique in her jazz classes.

Teaching Activity

Cuyjet's teaching specialization was ballet, yet her expertise in Luigi's jazz dance technique enabled her to become a sought-after jazz dance teacher in Philadelphia from 1957 to 1968. In addition to ballet and jazz, Cuyjet taught Dunham Technique, modern dance, ballroom dance, folk dance, children's dance, and beginning tap dance. Between 1948 and 1971, Cuyjet's primary teaching activity centered around her ballet classes at the Judimar School of Dance. Concurrent with her teaching responsibilities at Judimar, she taught for the Philadelphia recreation department (Wharton Recreation Center, 1948–49); local private dance studios; the Germantown Young Women's Christian Association (1948–49), the Yeadon, Pennsylvania recreation department (1949–50); and three area colleges, Delaware State College (1958–60), Cheyney State College (1958–60), and Maryland State College (MSC) (1957–71) (M.D. Cuyjet, Private Collection).

The Wharton Center, located at 22nd and Columbia Avenue in North Philadelphia, had established a dance program before Cuyjet arrived. Claude Marchant, a Dunham company dancer, was the center's first dance instructor. He left New York temporarily to teach in Philadelphia. Marchant taught a full schedule of Afro-Caribbean classes at the Wharton Center and when he left, Cuyjet was asked to replace him. There she taught Dunham Technique. She states: "I had a hard act to follow when I followed Claude Marchant. You always have a hard act to follow if there's been a male teacher teaching Afro-Caribbean" (personal communication, September 25, 1985). This was due to the predominance of women dance teachers and the novelty of the Afro-Caribbean dance vocabulary.

In the late 1950s to late 1960s, Cuyjet taught ballet, jazz, and modern dance at two private dance studios: the Jay Dash School of Dance and the Peter Kodel School of Dance. Both studios were located in the same building at 120 South 13th Street. These studios became desegregated in the late 1950s. (M.D. Cuyjet, Private Collection). Nancy Lynch, Cuyjet's folk dance teacher, introduced Cuyjet to Jay Dash. His specialty was tap dance, and his school served children and young adults. In the 1960s, Dash was a guest choreographer for Judimar's recitals.

The Philadelphia Chapters of Dance Masters of America and the National Association of Dance and Affiliated Artists, dance organizations of which Cuyjet was a member, invited her to lead ballet and jazz workshops at their conventions for students and teachers in the 1950s and 1960s. Cuyjet states that these organizations were predominantly white at that time (personal communication, November 29, 1984).

Cuyjet was a regular teacher for the Jay Dash tri-state dance conventions from 1958 to 1967. Dash sponsored his own yearly teacher/student conventions. Cuyjet reminisces about these conventions:

> My ballet classes would have fifty or sixty people. People would flock to the modern jazz. The jazz classes would average 160 people. We taught in ballrooms. We would take over the Adelphia Hotel—all three ballrooms. It would take us all afternoon to teach the pieces because they had to come up fifty at a time so we could do the same step over again. (personal communication, November 29, 1984)

Cuyjet's association with various dance organizations provided a very important network for reaching the larger Philadelphia dance community. In the late 1950s, interaction between Black and white dance education communities became a more frequent occurrence than in previous times.

Cuyjet taught dance in higher education through her work at three historically Black Colleges in the tri-state area: Delaware State College, presently Delaware State University, Dover, Delaware, Cheyney State College, presently Cheyney University of Pennsylvania, Cheyney, Pennsylvania and Maryland State College (MSC) presently, University of Maryland at Eastern Shore, Princess Anne, Maryland. She taught ballet and children's dance at Delaware State College, and directed Cheyney College's modern dance group (M.D. Cuyjet, Private Collection).

Cuyjet's Judimar performing unit presented a concert at MSC in 1957 at the invitation of Professor Thomas, an associate of Stephen Cuyjet's and a faculty member of the college. The president of the college, John Taylor Williams, was impressed with Judimar's presentation and asked Cuyjet to teach at the college. Cuyjet states: "I took my little company to perform and I never left. I stayed there fourteen years. The president of the college was very enamored with this ballet company—as he called it" (personal communication, September 11, 1985).

Cuyjet taught ballet, jazz, modern dance, and dance history in the physical education department at MSC. Before Cuyjet arrived, the physical education instructors were responsible for all the dance courses. Cuyjet states:

> There was always a big quarrel through the fourteen years I was there. Every time they had a new physical education teacher we had to decide who would teach what [dance courses]. Most of the physical education teachers were modern dance long shots—there should not have been a problem. I was ballet and jazz. (personal communication, September 11, 1985)

Cuyjet's teaching schedule included eight o'clock morning dance classes on Mondays and Tuesdays. On Monday afternoons and evenings, Cuyjet offered dance classes for the community. These classes catered to children and young adults. Many of the students were children of MSC faculty members. Cuyjet's community outreach program eventually developed into the Princess Anne branch of Judimar. The remainder of the week, Cuyjet devoted her time to her Philadelphia school (M.D. Cuyjet, personal communication, September 11, 1985).

Williams was supportive of Cuyjet's school and he invited her Philadelphia Judimar branch to present annual campus concerts. He also arranged for the college's public relations department to secure additional performance dates at local elementary and high schools. Maryland State College served as a very important testing ground for some of Judimar's performance pieces. Cuyjet staged *Giselle* there in 1960, before presenting it in Philadelphia.

Each year Cuyjet organized a college production. The cast included advanced dancers from the school and community and Judimar dancers. In 1968 Cuyjet directed and choreographed her most ambitious collegiate collaboration: *Go Now, Pay Later,* a musical production for MSC's choir and band, augmented with Judimar dancers.

Cuyjet admits that dividing her time between the college and her Philadelphia school was taxing, but states that it was worth it because of the teaching and production experiences. In addition, Cuyjet's affiliation with MSC enabled her to send her daughter, Judy, and son, Stephen, Jr., to the college on scholarship. Cuyjet taught at Maryland State College until 1971. She speaks of her years at the college as one of the most cherished experiences of her career.

Pedagogical Foundation

Cuyjet's teaching specialization was ballet. This section will examine the basic teaching approach she utilized for this dance form from 1948 to 1971.

All of Cuyjet's teachers have influenced her teaching approach and she refers to their influence by saying: "I've gotten pearls from all of them" (personal communication, September 25, 1985). Cuyjet was by no means a carbon copy of the teachers with whom she studied. She borrowed the best from each. When Cuyjet discusses her training experiences, she mentions the fact that she did not always agree with each teacher's total teaching approach. For example, she is critical of teachers who give negative directives and states: "Instead of telling a student don't do, tell them what they should do" (personal communication, September 25, 1985).

Cuyjet has been trained in several systems of ballet and each utilizes a slightly different terminology and stylistic interpretation. She received a foundation in Cecchetti (Italian method) from Dorsey and Cannon, experience in the Russian or Vaganova school of training at Ballet Arts, and French and Russian preparation from George Chaffee (M.D. Cuyjet, personal communication, January 14, 1986).

When asked from which school of ballet she teaches she states: "I don't like to say that I come from a particular school. If forced I would say that I take the best of the Italian school (Cecchetti) and the Russian (Vaganova) with a dash of French" (personal communication, January 14, 1986). According to some of Cuyjet's former students (Judith Jamison and Donna Lowe Warren), she uses a combination of the Italian, Russian, and French ballet systems. According to Delores Browne Abelson, Cuyjet's methods are mainly based upon the Russian school of ballet (personal communication, August 23, 1985).

Many of Cuyjet's colleagues and former students mention her academic approach in preparing for her craft. Throughout her career she studied ballet pedagogy. During the Judimar era, she ordered ballet pedagogy books from *Dance Magazine* in order to keep abreast of the latest trends in teaching. In addition, she devoted a great deal of time to the study of ballet terminology and dance history (M.D. Cuyjet, personal communication, January 27, 1985). The teaching references she used between 1946–71 included *The Ballet Student's Primer*, by Kay Ambroise, *A Concise History of Ballet*, by Ferdinando Reyna, and *Principles of Classical Ballet*, by Agrippina Vaganova. After the Judimar era she used additional references such as *Classes in Classical Ballet*, by Asaf Messerer,

The Classic Ballet, by Muriel Stewart and Lincoln Kirstein, *Technique for the Ballet Dancer*, by Sylvia Hamer and *Ballet Studio*, by Ann Woolians (M.D. Cuyjet, personal communication, July 1, 1986).

Cuyjet had a reputation as a thorough disciplinarian. Her usual teaching temperament was direct and firm, with a touch of humor. Judith Jamison, Elmer Ball, Donna Lowe Warren, and Delores Browne Abelson, all former students, state that Cuyjet was extremely strict. According to Delores Browne Abelson, one of Judimar's students who pursued a career in ballet, Cuyjet set high performance and personal behavior expectations for all of her students. Abelson states: "She was very tough. She was specific about what she wanted in personal behavior as well as class performance. She addressed the whole person—hygiene, social behavior and so on. She was extremely particular about promptness. You were not admitted into class late" (personal communication, August 23, 1985). Judith Jamison states that Cuyjet used humor to break the tension in class, but Jamison often missed the punch line because she was concentrating so hard (personal communication, May 16, 1985).

Cuyjet attributes her teaching disposition to her upbringing and early dance training. She comments on her reputation as a demanding teacher by stating:

> I think it's my personality. My children were raised the same way. My mother did it to me. My aunt, my whole family were strict disciplinarians. My first teacher, Essie Marie, was also a strict disciplinarian, right down to the social graces. (personal communication, April 3, 1986)

In a 1974 *Philadelphia Inquirer* article Cuyjet comments on her teaching reputation: "I feel I was such an intense teacher because I was going to have someone else do the dancing I could never do" (Sims, 1974. n.p.).

Fundamental Teaching Approach

Cuyjet's teaching approach placed emphasis on placement, body alignment, and correct usage and pronunciation of ballet terminology and performance. Her interest in body alignment began as a student with Essie Marie Dorsey. Dorsey stressed the importance of proper body alignment to guard against injury. She observed each student closely for anatomical constraints. Dorsey's keen understanding of basic anatomy and biomechanics enabled her to correctly evaluate Cuyjet's limited spinal range of motion. Cuyjet's later spinal injury was a result of stress placed on her inflexible spine. Cuyjet states:

> We were creating a formation for an acrobatic routine and Dorsey noticed that I was encountering difficulty in bending backwards. She came over to me and gently ran her fingers along my spine. She whispered to me never to put myself in a formation that required a full back bend again because the vertebrae of my spine were extremely close together and she felt them "crunch" when I was attempting to bend backwards. She told me my spine could not take the stress. (personal communication, September 11, 1985)

Thomas Cannon and George Chaffee encouraged Cuyjet to consider fundamental elements of kinesiology and biomechanics in regards to execution and body alignment in ballet. The training she received from Dorsey, Cannon, and Chaffee underscored the importance of proper placement of the feet, legs, pelvis, torso, arms, and head as essential to movement efficiency and in achieving a pleasing classical body line.

Cuyjet placed a premium on her students' knowledge of ballet terminology. Warren states: "Cuyjet was big on learning terminology. Since ballet terms are all French, we were expected to understand movement directions in that language" (D.L. Warren, personal communication, September 28, 1985). Cuyjet held vocabulary sessions during class. "When the blackboard came out, we had to be prepared to spell, read, and associate vocabulary with movement. She was a total educator" (D.B. Abelson, personal communication, August 23, 1985).

In addition to vocabulary sessions, Cuyjet's students were required to keep dance scrapbooks. Cuyjet comments:

> We encouraged parents to give their children a subscription to *Dance Magazine*. We would refer to the magazine during class when discussing famous dancers, or body line. We always had a frame of reference. There were special assignments on Black dancers. One involved compiling two pages on Asadata Dafora, the dancer who introduced African dance to the United States concert stage. (personal communication, April 3, 1986)

The blackboard sessions and scrapbook assignments suggest that Cuyjet's academic approach to learning her craft influenced her teaching approach.

Cuyjet strongly believed that performance should be addressed in dance classes. She insisted that her students be cognizant of the fact that performing is related to courage. According to Cuyjet, performing in front of an audience is a courageous undertaking. She also told students that choosing the appropriate performance energy is paramount to communicating effectively with the audience. Cuyjet states: "If you are dancing for a house with a balcony, you should use your eyes to direct the energy up and out. If you are dancing in a space without a balcony the focus is straight out" (personal communication, April 3, 1986).

Judith Jamison states that performance was a major element of her dance preparation with Cuyjet.

> Marion did not speak to us of projection and dynamics; she told us to dance. She made us aware of ourselves as dancers—that regardless of where we were on stage, no matter if you were the last kid in the back row, you danced just as you danced when you were front, stage center. At Judimar we did not just execute exercises in the studio; we danced at the barre and center. Everything was for the stage. (Maynard, 1982, p. 21)

Cuyjet composed her own syllabus and taught in phases or units. Each class level was expected to cover a certain amount of material. She introduced pointe work when her students reached the age of ten. She taught from lesson plans. "I memorize the plan and place it on the piano, if I need to refer to it" (personal communication, April 3, 1986).

Cuyjet gradually introduced new class material. She always made sure the students were comfortable with ongoing class work before introducing new material. She comments on teaching intermediate and advanced classes versus beginning classes:

> The higher levels already know the barre work, and the criticism is conversational. We discuss breathing patterns on certain movements, and I remind students to be cautious of their old habits, [chin out, and so on]. We talk about things they need to watch. One area is misplacing energy. They already know the foundation, we talk about particulars. In the lower classes we are still teaching the bread and butter material [piqué turns, arabesque line, working on achieving a pure classical line]. (personal communication, April 3, 1986)

Cuyjet delivered material in class by demonstrating and used a "hands on" method of correcting. She gently manipulated a student's body so they would be able to feel the proper alignment. She frequently used imagery for corrections and to indicate dynamics (D.L. Warren, personal communication, September 28, 1985).

She used her voice as a teaching tool, a technique she admired in Dokoudowsky's teaching. Cuyjet states:

> I use my voice a lot to change dynamics or phrasing. I use it to keep the power and momentum, especially when coaching the men. I also use my voice to sing the rhythm for a movement combination, so the pianist can choose the right music for it. (personal communication, April 3, 1986)

The interviews conducted with Cuyjet's former students and colleagues did not yield primary information regarding her specific teaching approach. However, data regarding their most memorable recollections of Cuyjet's ballet classes coupled with observations of Cuyjet's teaching indicate that her fundamental teaching approach was both academic and performance-oriented. She provided opportunities for students to gain knowledge of basic historical and theoretical aspects of ballet technique. Concurrent with this was an emphasis on expressive performance. Execution with "feeling" was imperative.

Two aspects of Cuyjet's classes were musicality and individual attention. She stressed the importance of "dancing with the music," and her extensive knowledge of classical ballet's musical standards enabled her to prescribe the appropriate music for specific movement phrases or combinations. During class she gave a great deal of individual student corrections. Donna Lowe Warren states: "Cuyjet was very observant. She saw everything. We thought she had eyes in the back of her head" (personal communication, September 28, 1985). Cuyjet monitored her students' progress very closely regardless of their level of technical proficiency. She familiarized herself with each student's strengths and weaknesses and gave consistent feedback.

Documentation and Analysis of a Ballet Class: Structure and Delivery

This section will be divided into three descriptive sections. The first is a generic description of the basic type of ballet class Cuyjet taught between 1948 and 1971. It is based upon my observations of Cuyjet teaching class, interviews with her, my own knowledge of ballet class procedure, and reference information from *Ballet Basics*, by Sandra Noll Hammond. It is a prototypical ballet class rather than any particular session.

The second section will follow the same format as the previous description. (Definitions for ballet terms used in this section are located in Appendix A—Glossary of Ballet Terms.) It is a detailed verbal description as recounted by Cuyjet. The barre work consists of a core of fundamental exercises. Cuyjet varies this repertory in each class by adding movements. The adagio combinations remain the same until students perfect them. New allegro and across the floor combinations are assigned for each class.

The third segment is my description and analysis of Cuyjet teaching a company class for the Philadelphia Dance Company (Philadanco) on July 1, 1986. Occasional reference will be made to observations of Cuyjet teaching Philadanco January 14, 1986, and a children's professional class at the Philadelphia School of Dance Arts, March 25, 1986.

Cuyjet states that her teaching approach in the 1980s is extremely similar to the manner in which she taught during the Sydney-Marion and Judimar eras. She continues to place emphasis on placement, body alignment, correct usage and pronunciation of ballet terminology, and performance. The primary difference is that she is unable to demonstrate completely ("full out") because of anatomical constraints. The spinal operation she underwent in 1968, resulted in a shifted pelvis and a laterally curved spine. Since her ability to demonstrate standing up is limited, she uses her arms, hands, legs, and feet to demonstrate while sitting down and verbal directives, in addition to "marking" the movement standing.

I: Ballet Class Prototype

The class is organized into three main sections: barre work, center floor, and across the floor movement.

BARRE WORK. Students perform their exercises while holding with one or both hands onto a wooden barre attached to the walls of the room. Sometimes portable barres are placed in the center of the floor. Barre exercises are geared toward increasing strength and flexibility in the feet, ankles, legs, arms, back, and hip socket. The barre work is designed to help the dancer attain balance and control and to gain speed in the feet, lightness in the legs and to stabilize turnout (outward rotation of the hip ball-and-socket joint). Barre work is most often referred to as the "mechanics" of ballet technique (Hammond, 1974, p. 45).

CENTER FLOOR. Students stand in horizontal rows in the center of the studio and execute barre work in combination with arm, head, leg, and shoulder movements. Attention is given to flow of energy, spatial awareness, balance, musicality, and classical body alignment. It consists of two main parts: allegro (lively, rapid, steps that include jumps), and adagio (lyrical movement combinations which include port de bras, classical ballet positions of the body, line poses of arabesque, attitude, and pirouettes) (Hammond, 1974, p. 80).

ACROSS THE FLOOR. Students perform locomotor movement combinations from one side of the room to the other. They travel horizontally across the floor in duets, trios, or quartets. The work concentrates on aerial, jumping, and turning movements, such as leaps, tour jetés, and waltz turns.

II: Ballet Class Description as recounted by Marion Cuyjet on April 3, 1986.

BARRE WORK.

1. *Demi-Plié; Relevé; Warm-up.* With both hands on the barre students face the barre and stand in first position. Demi-plié, force the instep out, then stretch legs till the body rises to a relevé. Then press the heels to the floor. Reverse the movement. Repeat the exercise in second position.
2. *Ankle Flex and Rotations.* With the left hand on the barre and body facing wall that is perpendicular to the barre, stand in fifth position. Demi-plié, then battement degagé right leg sharply, and straighten both legs at the same time. Flex right ankle, then execute an outward ankle rotation 360°, reverse the rotation inward 360° and stop. Stretch the right foot to tendu in fourth position front and close to fifth position demi-plié. Repeat the exercise en croix (to the side and to the back). The entire exercise is repeated on the left side, right hand holding the barre.

3. *Demi-Plié and Grande Plié.* (preparation for pointe work) From first position, left hand on the barre, execute two demi-pliés, relevé and balance, lower heels to the floor. Follow this with two grande pliés. Then with right arm porte de bras, cambré away then into the barre. Finish the exercise on relevé sous sus in fifth position, both arms off the barre held in second position. The exercise is repeated in second, third, fourth, and fifth position. Turn to the left side, right hand holding the barre and execute the entire exercise.
4. *Tendu.* From fifth position, left hand on the barre, execute two tendus to the front with the right leg and foot, then three battement tendu jeté closing fifth each time. Repeat the exercise en croix. The entire exercise is repeated on the other side with the right hand holding the barre.

   The tendu set is done in two versions. One is long and deliberate for the advanced classes and the other is short for the children and pre-teens.
5. *Ronde de jambe.* (This exercise is usually combined with leg extensions) Left hand is on the barre. From first position, ronde de jambe en dehors with right leg eight times. Finish the eighth rotation by swinging the leg into the air to the front of the body, then porte en l'air to second position and gently fold the leg into retiré and relevé balance. (The variation is as follows: after the eighth rotation, swing the leg to the front and grande ronde de jambe to the back, balancoire the leg to the front, porte en l'air to second position, then retiré and balance.) Repeat the combination, en dedans. Turn to the other side and repeat.
6. *Frappé.* (Two types are executed: frappé jeté and frappé-tendu) From sur-le-cou-de-pied, frappe-jeté right foot to second position three times. Finish with one double frappé-jeté. Repeat four times. Then execute the same exercise with the frappé tendu. Turn to the

other side and repeat. This exercise can be mixed with petite battements.

7. *Fondu with Developpé.* From fifth position, with left hand on the barre, the right leg moves to second position, en l'air. Then fondu developpé front, fondu developpé to second then again to the back. Repeat desired number of times. Turn to the other side and repeat.

   The beginning classes are not ready for fondu developpé. Instead it is executed in stages. From fifth position demi-plié, the right foot moves through sur-le-cou-de-pied, retiré, attitude front, straightens to a front extension, then the leg lowers and finishes in fifth position demi-plié. The exercise is done en croix.

8. *Ronde de Jambe en L'air.* From first position, left hand on the barre, right leg moves to second position en l'air. Execute the ronde de jambe en l'air en dedans and en dehors. This exercise is sometimes mixed with fouetté and pirouettes.

9. *Échappé.* This movement is included to accelerate the tempo of the class. Échappé is done in combination with movement exercises that have already been executed. For advanced classes it is executed on pointe.

10. *Changements and Entrechats.* Facing the barre, both hands holding the barre for support. These elevation movements are executed from fifth position demi-plié.

    During this phase of class Cuyjet tells a story of how King Louis XIV and his dance masters developed the entrechat series. The result is a mini dance history lesson presented in dramatization. She delivers the scenario to beginner, intermediate, and advanced classes.

11. *Allegro at the Barre.* (Changements and entrechats in combinations)

Cuyjet teaches allegro at the barre before having students execute it in the center. "We can't teach allegro center floor until they get control over it."

12. *Barre Stretches.* The barre stretch involves placing one leg at a time on the barre and executing exercises that will increase flexibility of the lumbar spine region of the back, hamstrings, and gracilis muscles. Certain stretches are risky. To teach them correctly student teachers help Cuyjet assist with "hands on" placement and body alignment.

The barre phase of class is between 45 minutes to an hour long.

CENTER FLOOR.

1. *Warm-up.* Facing the mirror in fifth position, tendu to second position then close back to fifth position traveling backwards. Reverse and travel forward.
2. *Adagio.* The adagio is always simple for beginner students and more difficult for advanced students. It includes arabesque poses, port de bras, pirouettes, and positions of the body.
3. *Allegro.* Allegro work is done if time permits. For the advanced classes this portion of class is sometimes devoted to partnering, female pointe work or male elevation work.

Center work is around 15 minutes long.

ACROSS THE FLOOR.

1. Long movement combinations are executed from one side of the room to the other. The across the floor movement combinations are the most dance like phase of class. It is a culminating activity which is a synthesis of the entire class.

Across the floor work is around 15 minutes long.

III: Ballet Class Description and Analysis by Melanye White Dixon

The following is a description of Cuyjet teaching company class for Philadanco, where she taught from the mid-1980s to the early 1990s. Before her teaching assignment began with the company she audited a few ballet classes at Pennsylvania Ballet's School in the Fairmont section of North Philadelphia in order to prepare to teach professional level dancers.

Philadanco is located at 9 North Preston Street in West Philadelphia and it shares the building with the Philadelphia School of Dance Arts. Both dance organizations are under the direction of Joan Myers Brown. Company class is held on the second floor in the main dance studio. Entrance into the studio is by way of a narrow hallway-sitting room. The floor is covered with deep lavender, low pile carpet. The light gray walls are lined with bulletin boards announcing Philadanco and city dance events.

The dancers enter the studio slowly, one at a time. Some sit while others stand and execute low energy whole-body warm-up exercises such as lateral torso stretches and forward body bends from the waist. The pianist enters and goes to the piano that is placed in the front left corner of the studio. He begins a perusal of his music for class. Cuyjet enters with a brisk walk. She is dressed all in white. She wears a sweat shirt, straight legged jeans, and soft leather jazz shoes. Her accessories include orange, circular, clip earrings and a gold chain necklace. Her hair is blonde. It is worn in a short layered style that sweeps away from her face. Her eyes scan the space. She leaves the room and returns with a chair which she places next to the piano and sits down. She removes from her dance bag a clip board, with her lesson plans attached, and places it on her lap. She reviews the lesson briefly and checks to see who is in attendance. Then she engages in a conversation with two male dancers who are stretching on the floor in front of her.

Class begins at 1:00 p.m. By this time there are seven students, four women and three men. Cuyjet states: "Okay, let's begin. Face the barre in first position." Each dancer immediately stops his or her warm up activity and finds a space at the barre that has been placed in the center of the studio or at the barre along the back and side walls. Cuyjet lights a cigarette and begins to smoke before reciting the first exercise. She instructs the class to begin with their usual demi-plié relevé exercise (as described in Section II). She gives the cue to the pianist to begin by stating: "preparation." During the exercise Cuyjet watches the class with intense concentration. She sits erect with her chin slightly raised. Her face is expressionless. Her arms are folded over the clip board. After the exercise is completed she gets up and walks to the rosin box in the far right of the studio. She applies a small amount of rosin to the bottom of her shoes and returns to her chair.

Cuyjet demonstrates the next exercise (ankle flex rotation, as described in Section II) with her right foot while sitting down. The next few barre exercises concentrate on strengthening the feet and ankles and stretching the achilles tendon. She demonstrates by using her arms and hands. Throughout, her demeanor is low-keyed and tone of voice is soft. She occasionally cautions the dancers to be aware of the turn-out in their hip sockets. In addition, she strikes her hands together in a single clap to indicate if a movement should be executed with a strong musical accent.

Cuyjet demonstrates a ronde de jambe exercise using her arms. She gives the dancers a pointer on correct execution: "The heel is delivered first." When the exercise is completed Cuyjet compliments their work. She smiles and states: "Nice, very, very, nice." The remainder of the barre exercises consist of frappés, fondu developpés, and barre stretches. These exercises accelerate in complexity and require more energy to execute than the previous exercises. When the dancers encounter problems remembering the movements, Cuyjet softly sings the terminology along with the melody of the music.

The pianist assisting Cuyjet has been working with her for the past year. He always plays the exact rhythms she requests. For example, before a porte de bras exercise she states: "I want it to swing like this." She demonstrates by swirling her right arm in front of her body in a horizontal figure eight formation using a waltz tempo. She counts the meter aloud as she demonstrates. The pianist then plays the appropriate music.

Cuyjet gives the dancers a short break. She looks down at her pad then looks up and states: "Barre stretches are coming up next." Most of the dancers look slightly fatigued and are perspiring moderately. They begin stretching (standing and on the floor), their legs to prepare for the coming set of exercises. The dancers do not acknowledge each other. There is silence. Cuyjet reviews her notes in preparation for the barre stretches. She begins smoking. It is as if the cigarette has been transformed into her "thinking prop." She takes out her pen, makes a few notes, then looks at her watch. Five minutes have passed. Sensing that the dancers have had ample time to rest and stretch, she summons the class to begin again: "Ready, okay, let's go."

Cuyjet instructs the dancers to execute the "regular barre stretch." They assume their starting position. The right leg is extended with the heel resting on the barre. The supporting leg is on the floor beneath the pelvis. The dancers bend their torsos forward toward the leg on the barre then reverse the bending action with a backward arch. She sings the movements as they execute them. Cuyjet begins to walk around the room to individually check the dancers. She cautions them not to "sink" into their supporting hip. She adjusts a male dancer's alignment while helping him find his balance during the backward arch. When the exercise is finished Cuyjet gives additional corrections to the same young man she assisted earlier. She asks him to repeat a portion of the exercise (a sous sus in relevé). The other dancers observe. His task is to transfer his weight from second position relevé to sous sus relevé. Cuyjet gently touches the gracilis muscle of his left thigh and states: "Press the inside muscles." He successfully completes the movement. She pats him on his back and praises him. He smiles with satisfaction.

Cuyjet compliments the entire class after the barre stretch is repeated with the left leg on the barre. She smiles, applauds and states: "No snaps, no jerks, no diversions at all." The next exercise is an allegro at the barre. Cuyjet returns to her chair. She verbalizes the movement combination while she demonstrates with her feet. The combination is as follows: jeté coupé, pas de bourreé to second position, brisé, balancoire, battu coupé, pas de bourreé to fifth position. Then she verbally walks them through the exercise, using an energetic four/four rhythm. Before they execute the movement without her assistance Cuyjet asks if there are any questions. There is no response from the dancers. Cuyjet states: "Okay, do it four times straight through." Afterward a female dancer asks for further clarification. Cuyjet goes over to her and demonstrates the exercise without the jumping movements. The dancer nods her head to indicate that she now understands. Cuyjet comments on their performance: "I want to see smoother phrasing. Marry the steps together. Remember, this exercise uses a small range of space." The dancers nod their heads to indicate that they understand her comments. They repeat the exercise but never perfect it. Cuyjet refrains from bestowing praise. She states in a humorous, sarcastic, tone: "Okay, we have to move on." The dancers respond with gentle laughter.

The time is 2:08. The barre portion of class is complete. The dancers place the barre that is in the center of the studio to the side of the room. Some of the dancers exit for water and quickly return. Cuyjet turns the lights on and goes to her chair to study her notes. She gestures for the dancers to come to the center of the floor. She verbally walks them through an adagio combination. It consists of selected movements from the barre phase of class, with added porte de bras, arabesque piqués, and a grande plié from first position. Cuyjet asks: "Do you remember this combination? My computer [referring to a female dancer with uncanny movement memory] over there remembers." The dancers learn the movement combination. They are familiar with it because it is from a previous class.

Prior to this phase of class the atmosphere is subdued and fairly informal. Cuyjet changes the mood. She raises the volume of her voice and her disposition becomes energetic and lighthearted. After the entire class executes the adagio combination, Cuyjet comments: "Umph, very nice, everybody feel all right? You look fine." She then divides the class into male and female groups. Cuyjet applauds after each group completes the combination.

It is now 2:15 p.m. The final phase of the class is across the floor movement. The men and women are given different combinations. The men perform first. They listen intently as Cuyjet recites their combination from her notes. It consists primarily of jumps and tours (turns) in the air. It is as follows: brisé, volé, glissade, assemblé, jeté attitude, chassé, tour de basque, step close back, tour l'air. Cuyjet calls Carlos Shorty, Philadanco's lead male dancer, to demonstrate while she guides him through the combination. The others look on. Shorty travels from the right side of the studio to the left. When the combination is finished he walks back to the right side of the studio to rejoin the other male dancers. They all perform the combination in a diamond shaped group formation across the floor. After their execution, Cuyjet praises them with applause.

Cuyjet briefly reviews her notes and asks the women to come to center floor. Their combination consists of a series of aerial movements and turns (tour jetés, chainés turns, piqué arabesque movements). Cuyjet requests a waltz tempo. She joins the dancers center floor and she reads and demonstrates the exercise as they follow. Cuyjet returns to her chair to watch them perform alone. As soon as they finish she states: "Use the music, ladies. Really milk it. Prima ballerina it!" Cuyjet's attitude is very lively. The dancers repeat the across the floor movement to Cuyjet's satisfaction.

Class ends in the center of the studio with a reverence improvisation. The dancers perform porte de bras movements to a short classical musical accompaniment. When they finish, class is dismissed. The dancers applaud Cuyjet to thank her for class.

Before the dancers leave the studio Cuyjet states: "This is my last class of the summer session with you. I have learned so much about relating to people and teaching through my experiences with you."

The teaching approach Cuyjet utilizes with Philadanco is of a coaching nature. Inasmuch as the dancers are professional, Cuyjet serves as a facilitator to help them refine their balletic technical and performance skills. For example, during both the Philadanco classes I observed (January 14, and July 1, 1986), Cuyjet encourages the dancers to execute smooth transitions between movements and movement phrases in order to achieve an even flow of energy. She urges them to "Marry the steps together." In another instance Cuyjet uses phrases like "I need some more drama"; "prima ballerina it"; "apply some 'stuff to it"—in order to motivate the female dancers to become more expressive during the adagio and across-the-floor work. During the January 14th class, Cuyjet mimicked a ballerina with a heavy Russian accent while explaining the appropriate performance energy for a female adagio combination. Her "performance" is used to inspire their performance.

In a 1986 interview, Cuyjet comments on her approach to teaching performance technique to Philadanco dancers:

> We take the bread-and-butter movements. We sell ourselves. We make our endings in the second balcony. We build the eyes into the movement. In a good ballet class, you work with the whole head and shoulders. Part of the head is the eyes.

She goes on to assert that even in classical ballet that Black dancers have a special way of moving.

> Black dancers have a tremendous amount of very deliberate energy. I see the same thing in Black basketball players. Even when they are doing very controlled things, they have so much energy.
>
> In today's class, I told the dancers to watch the white girl (Deanna Murphy) to see how she stretches into every step. The Black dancers move -out- to it (the new step), but they will use their energy in a different way. They are used to going -up-, not stretching -out. (Fox, April 6, 1986, pp. cc6-cc7)

The observation of Cuyjet teaching a children's professional class (ages 9–13), at the Philadelphia School of Dance Arts reveals that Cuyjet places more emphasis on fundamental principles of ballet technique when working with an advanced beginning class level. In addition, the disciplinary side of her teaching personality becomes clearly evident. She consistently gives corrections in a firm and exacting manner. In a stern tone, she reprimands the students for occasional moments of inattentiveness.

I conducted informal interviews with a few of the students from the classes I observed. I asked them to tell me what was special about Cuyjet's teaching approach. Here are some of the responses from the professional children's class: "She means business." "She really cares." "She scolds us sometimes, but always says, I still love you afterwards."

All the Philadanco dancers agree that Cuyjet provides an abundance of background information on the history and craft of ballet. For example, she frequently gives them informational handout sheets which cover ballet terminology, historical background on ballet technique, tips on correct execution and written descriptions of certain movement combinations from classes. Occasionally Cuyjet conducts brief "teaching sessions" for those Philadanco dancers who also teach. Although Cuyjet's approach varies according to the class level she teaches, the factor that remains constant is her commitment to nurturing technically proficient, well informed, and expressive dancers.

Cuyjet began her independent teaching career as a novice teacher. Her determined spirit propelled her toward a substantive quest to improve her teaching skills. Philadelphia dance educators Thomas Cannon and John Hines assisted Cuyjet in her efforts to become a renowned teacher. Cannon tutored her in theory and studio work and Hines advised her to travel to New York City for advanced training. Cuyjet developed her capabilities as an advanced-level ballet teacher and augmented her technical training with independent research in dance history and theory.

Cuyjet's forte was ballet, yet she valued contemporary and ethnic techniques. She studied jazz, modern, and Afro-Caribbean dance forms and as a result she emerged as a versatile and marketable dance educator.

Cuyjet maintained an active teaching schedule. She taught at her own school (Judimar), local private schools, recreation and community centers and at three predominately Black colleges in the tri-state area. Cuyjet encountered a wide range of teaching experiences and with each assignment her commitment to providing dance preparation to children in the Black community grew.

Cuyjet was a strict disciplinarian and thorough teacher. She exemplified the "old school" ballet instructor and her fundamental teaching approach was academic and performance oriented. She was intent on nurturing students who excelled as technicians and performers. Her exemplary teacher status was due to her teaching ability and in part to her intense dedication to grooming Black children in classical ballet, a dance form traditionally considered closed to African Americans.

Cuyjet's teaching approach created a stellar tradition of dance training for which Judimar was renowned. By continuing her dance studies throughout most of her career, she enhanced her teaching skills and enriched the dance lives of her students by sharing the knowledge gleaned from ballet masters in New York and Philadelphia. Her teaching style was loving, yet exacting, and she provided all her students with a positive vision of their capabilities. The force of her pedagogical philosophy pervaded structure of her dance studio. The Judimar School of Dance will be examined in a subsequent chapter.

CHAPTER 3

Judimar Era (1948–1971)

The State of Black Philadelphia

Like all performing and visual arts, dance exists in the context of its socio-cultural milieu. Therefore, social and political realities must be taken into consideration in the assessment of the arts. The purpose of this chapter is to provide an historical frame of reference for the era from which Cuyjet emerged.

Cuyjet's career developed during the post-World War II era of the 1950s and continued through the 1960s. During this period, Black Philadelphians joined the national movement to improve the quality of life for Black Americans. Black Philadelphia continued to struggle for better economic and educational opportunities, increased political power, racial harmony, and adequate social and cultural outlets.

Some of the self-help organizations which were active in addressing the economic, educational, political, and social needs of Black Philadelphia were the Philadelphia Urban League; the Educational Equality League; the National Association for the Advancement of Colored People; The Peace Mission Movement; The Young Women's Christian Association; The Young Men's Christian Association, and the Heritage House ("Black Achievement," 1963, pp. 23–24). The *Philadelphia Tribune*, America's oldest Black Newspaper, was influential in mounting an effective campaign to increase political awareness and promote social change (Franklin, 1979, p. xviii).

The Great Migration lost momentum during the 1930s, but during World War II and the post-war years, the number of African Americans migrating from the South to Philadelphia increased (Du Bois, 1967, p. xxix). By 1970, Blacks accounted for 33.5% of Philadelphia's population (Mondesire, 1984, p. 1). From the late 1940s to early 1970s, most Black Philadelphians resided in either South, North Central, or West Philadelphia (Du Bois, 1967, p. xxxiii). Each of the regions was inhabited by Blacks and whites, but their communities were separated due to residential segregation (Hershberg, 1981, p. 17). South Philadelphia was the first area where large numbers of Blacks settled; next was North Philadelphia, then West Philadelphia. The following quote suggests that Blacks were attracted to North and West Philadelphia because of better housing.

> ...In the years following World War II, middle income whites left North and West Philadelphia for new single-family housing in the city's "Greater Northeast" and the surrounding suburbs. Blacks left older, high-density neighborhoods closer to the city's center and occupied the more desirable housing vacated by these whites. (Yancy & Ericksen, 1979, pp. 253–262)

Economics

Economic conditions in Black Philadelphia before 1940 were grim. High unemployment plagued Black Philadelphia since the late 1920s (Franklin, 1979, pp. 105–127). Racial discrimination in hiring was a major problem. Manufacturing, the life blood of Philadelphia's economy before the 1950s, excluded Blacks. Hershberg (1981) states:

> Although Blacks continued to live in and near areas characterized by high industrial concentration, they were excluded from industrial work. Despite the fact that eighty percent of Black Philadelphians lived within one mile of 5,000 industrial jobs, less than thirteen percent of the Black force found gainful employment in manufacturing. (Hershberg, 1981, p. 15)

Most Black Philadelphians worked in menial, domestic, and unskilled occupations. There was constant competition for industrial jobs with Italian, German, and Irish ethnic groups (Hershberg, 1981, p. 15). During World War II and the post-war years, employment opportunities improved slightly (Du Bois, 1967, p. xxxviii).

Ironically, discrimination in industry began to decrease as the manufacturing jobs left the city. "Just when the worst racist hiring practices in industry eased, there was a suburbanization of manufacturing activity" (Hershberg, 1981, p. 16).

In the 1950s and 1960s, there were increasing job opportunities in skilled, white collar, and professional occupations. Still, racist hiring practices continued to exist and Black Philadelphians were more likely to work at jobs which offered limited upward mobility (Mathis, 1981, p. 163). The demand for increased employment opportunities justifiably came from the Black community. Black Philadelphia's religious leaders galvanized the community to campaign for improvements. An example of a successful campaign during the 1960s was the Selective Patronage Program, spearheaded by 400 Baptist ministers. Selected businesses and industries were encouraged to revise their hiring policies toward Blacks. If the company refused to comply with the program's request, the ministers encouraged their congregations to boycott their products and services. Programs were developed in conjunction with the Selective Patronage Program to prepare people to qualify for jobs as they became available (Saunders, 1966, pp. 25–26).

Most Black-owned businesses struggled for survival during the post-war years through the 1950s. One of the major problems was attracting private capital investment. In response to this dilemma, the U.S. government established the Minority Enterprise Small Business Investment Company in the 1960s. This organization was specifically designed to provide a form of venture capital to stimulate minority business development (Bowser, p. 114). By 1964, there were 4,000 Black-owned businesses in Black Philadelphia. The majority of these were categorized as small or marginal (Du Bois, 1967, p. l).

Education

Improving public school education and providing quality vocational and community education programs has historically been a major concern in Black Philadelphia. Although informal desegregation was initiated after 1932, the struggle to abolish official public school segregation ended in 1940. Most Black Philadelphians strongly believed that a segregated school system was a primary obstacle to economic, political, social, and educational advancement (Franklin, 1979, pp. 128–150). By 1950, the population of Philadelphia's public school system was overwhelmingly Black. These students inherited a troubled school system. Dilapidated buildings, inadequate and antiquated facilities, financial instability, and overcrowding were major concerns (Franklin, 1979, p. 200).

In the 1950s and 1960s, there was a movement to improve the Philadelphia school system with the assistance of federal funds. Black teachers and administrators began to develop strategies to increase educational achievement. Changes resulted, but the school system failed to address fundamental literacy skills (Franklin, 1979, pp. 199–144).

The Berean Institute was an example of a predominately Black vocational institution which supplied quality educational programs since 1899. It prepared students for careers in electronics, business administration, secretarial science, auto mechanics, and tailoring (Franklin, 1979, p. 171). Community education programs funded by federal anti-poverty grants targeted social advancement, community development, juvenile delinquency, and interracial cooperation as primary areas of concern (Franklin, 1979, pp. 87–101).

Politics

Political activity in Black Philadelphia escalated in the late 1940s. Most of the political impetus before World War II focused on litigation to desegregate

Philadelphia's public schools (Franklin, 1979, pp. 128–150). Black Philadelphia's party affiliation was Republican until the 1930s. The meager gains made in politics were achieved with the assistance of the Black Philadelphia Citizens Republican Club (Ballard, 1984, p. 208).

In the 1950s and 1960s, Black Philadelphia supported the Democratic machine, yet the party failed to address the economic, political, and educational advancement of Black Philadelphia (Franklin, 1979, p. 202). Vincent Franklin comments on the pitfalls of the one-party orientation.

> The pattern of Black participation in local politics in the 1950s, 1960s, and early 1970s, resembled that of the pre-1932 era when the Black vote was firmly attached to the Republican machine. One party orientation limited the need for the political establishment to make concessions on Black political demands since the Black vote was generally taken for granted by the Democratic politicians in power. (Franklin, 1979, p. 202)

There have been independent political factions which have existed in Black Philadelphia since the 1800s (Mathis, 1981, p. 64). The Civil Rights and Black Power movements of the 1960s stimulated the activities of several political organizations such as the Black People's Unity Movement (BPUM), the Republic of New Africa, Philadelphia's Chapter of the Student Non-violent Coordinating Committee, the Black Panthers, and the North City Congress (C.E. White, personal communication, November 22, 1985). In the 1950s and 1960s, protest activities such as boycotts and demonstrations directed toward changing municipal politics, proved to be more successful than organized political activity in resolving Black political demands (Franklin, 1979, p. 202).

Social and Cultural Life

Black Philadelphia's churches, fraternal orders, and civic and social clubs provided vital social and cultural outlets. The Elks and the Prince Hall Masons were fraternal orders which sponsored numerous social, cultural, and educational activities. The Philadelphia Pyramid Club and the Philadelphia Cotillion Society were additional leading organizations (Saunders, 1966, p. 16).

The majority of Black Philadelphians were working class (C.E. White, personal communication, November 22, 1985). Those who were employed as teachers and postal workers were considered members of the Black middle class. There was a small segment of the community that considered itself middle and upper middle class on the basis of skin color and place of origin. Many "Old Philadelphians" were a part of this group. The system of social and class stratification based on the color of skin and length of residence in Philadelphia lessened after World War II, but lingered through the 1970s (Ballard, 1984, pp. 198–201).

Modern Black Philadelphia experienced a fusion of Southern and Northern cultures. The outcome was a community which produced many successful performing and visual artists, writers, scholars, and athletes (Ballard, 1984, pp. 217–230). This list includes the following people: Henry Tanner, Meta Vaux Warrick, Barbara Chase Ribound, Marion Anderson, the Nicholas Brothers, Ethel Waters, McCoy Tyner, Jimmy Smith, Nina Simone, Alain Locke, Roy Campanella, and Wilt Chamberlain (Blockson, 1975, p. 2).

Race Relations

The racial climate in Philadelphia has been tense since the 1830s (Cazenave, January 23, 1985). Racial conflicts surfaced often and Franklin (1979, p. 195) states that the increase in the number of Blacks between 1900 and 1950 made racial conflicts more frequent. In March 1942, a Black family was driven from their newly purchased home in a white section of North Philadelphia by an angry mob of armed white residents (Franklin, 1979, p. 159). In 1944, the Philadelphia

Transit Company (PTC) went on strike because of the upgrading of PTC Black workers to streetcar motormen (Franklin, 1979, p. 160).

In the late 1940s, there was a proliferation of educational programs to promote interracial cooperation and improve Black/white relations. Racial tensions eased somewhat in the 1950s and 1960s due to interracial cooperation organizations. One such organization was the Fellowship Commission, a citywide community relations group composed of local social agencies and concerned citizens. The commission offered assistance in coordinating programs of constituent agencies, acted as a mediator in interracial problems, and conducted intercultural educational programs (Franklin, 1979, p. 157).

Black Philadelphia's Cultural Arts Organizations and Institutions

Black cultural arts organizations and institutions began to proliferate in the late 1940s. They were established in order to provide alternative outlets to the existing mainstream institutions that catered to European American cultural traditions. Black cultural arts organizations and institutions were founded on the premise that they would preserve African American culture and heritage and provide enrichment experiences in music, visual arts, theater, and dance (Doke, 1983, p. 31).

Philadelphia Concert Orchestra and the Dra Mu Opera Company

Two music organizations which developed were the Philadelphia Concert Orchestra and the Dra Mu Opera Company. Violinist Raymond Smith founded both organizations to provide instrumental and vocal performing opportunities in classical music in Black Philadelphia. The Philadelphia Concert Orchestra was established in the early 1940s and Smith used his own money to organize the orchestra. All of its members held jobs in other occupations (Schauensee, 1948, n.p.). Some were former members of the Philadelphia Anderson Orchestra which was organized in 1913 (Southern, 1971, p. 436). The orchestra presented at least two concerts a year (Schauensee, 1948).

The Dra Mu Opera Company was established in 1945. The nucleus of the company consisted of singers that Smith auditioned for the Philadelphia Concert Orchestra (Schauensee, 1948). Smith's main objective was to give African Americans the opportunity to sing opera and to cultivate an appreciation for grand opera in Black Philadelphia. The following statement of purpose was in the Dra Mu's 1948–49 season booklet:

> Dra Mu was founded because of the firm conviction that there was a gap in the cultural life of the community that it could fill. There was an awareness that a wealth of undiscovered talent whose full potentialities had not been revealed existed in the community. (M. Poindexter Sr., Private Collection)

Although Smith started the company on his own, a Dra Mu organization was eventually created. Auxiliary committees were formed to support fundraising endeavors (W. Smith, personal communication, October 14, 1985).

The Dra Mu's assistant director was W. Russell Johnson, the musical director was Henry Elkan, and Raymond Smith served as president and general manager. The chorus consisted of 40 to 50 singers (Schauensee, 1948, n.p.). Dra Mu members who later received international acclaim are Reginald Farrar and Wilhelminia Fernandez (W. Smith, personal communication, October 14, 1985).

Essie Marie Dorsey was the company's first ballet director and after World War II, Thomas Cannon assumed the post. Cuyjet's students performed as guest artists with the Dra Mu and the Philadelphia Concert Orchestra in the late 1940s and early 1950s (M.D. Cuyjet, Private Collection).

The company's repertory included *La Traviata*, *Carmen*, *Faust*, *Cavalleria Rutsicana*, *Tales of Hoffman*, *Hansel and Gretel*, and *Aida*. In 1950, Dra Mu staged composer Clarence Cameron Whites's *Ouanga*, an opera based on the Haitian leader Dessalines (Schauensee, 1950). The Dra Mu Opera Company remained in existence until 1960. Elizabeth Wilder, a Dra Mu principal, reorganized the company in 1975 (Tierney, 1975). The New Dra Mu dissolved in the late 1970s (M. Poindexter Jr., personal communication, August 28, 1985).

Heritage House

The Heritage House was the leading cultural arts institution in Black Philadelphia from 1954 until the mid-1970s. It was founded by Dr. Eugene Waymon Jones, educator, musician, and choral director. Jones was born in Moundsville, West Virginia, January 16, 1915. He received his B.S. degree in Education from Bluefield State College in 1938. Jones came to Philadelphia in 1940 to live with his uncle, Reverend Henry Pickney Jones, pastor of Mother Bethel AME Church. He served in the armed forces and returned to Philadelphia in 1945. He then received his Master's degree in Education from Temple University in 1948 and his Doctorate in Education from Temple in 1954. He taught at Berean Institute and at Temple University in the Department of Secondary Education (Giddens, 1986, p. 6). Jones, a prominent community activist, served on the executive board of the Philadelphia branch of the NAACP, on the board of directors of the Dra Mu Opera Company, was founder of the North Philadelphia Congress, and a member of the Fellowship Commission (Wanamaker, 1985, p. 44).

In 1949, Jones founded the Philadelphia Cotillion Society and one of its primary functions was community fundraising. The first year in existence the Society sponsored a Christmas Cotillion Ball at which debutantes were presented. The proceeds of the affair went to support the Mercy Douglass Hospital (see Plate 8).

The Christmas Cotillion became an annual event and the highlight of each ball was the presentation of a humanitarian award to an outstanding American. The award was called *The Cross of Malta.* Recipients of the award included Marion Anderson, Dr. Ralph Bunche, Jackie Robinson, Thurgood Marshall, Dr.

Martin Luther King, Jr., Eleanor Roosevelt, Branch Rickey, Joan Crawford, and Mary McLeod Bethune (see Plate 9). The Christmas Cotillion was a lavish spectacle which became a major event in Black Philadelphia and it received national exposure in *Life* Magazine, January 22, 1951 (Doke, 1983, p. 1983).

In addition to the presentation of debutantes and the *Cross of Malta,* each Christmas Cotillion featured a ballet production conceived and directed by Jones. He selected local dance educators to choreograph and one of the main purposes of the production was to showcase dancers in Black Philadelphia. Two exceptionally well received ballets were *Frozen Fire* (1950), and *The Blue Venus* (1955). The following excerpt is from a review of *The Blue Venus* which appeared in *The Afro-American*:

> The Christmas Cotillion presented the ballet spectacle *The Blue Venus* here before an audience of more than 6,000. The performance which was at Convention Hall, Philadelphia, made use of 7,000 dancers and many lavish costumes. This is believed to be the finest ballet given by the Cotillion to date. The story was by Eugene Waymon Jones. The ballet direction and choreography was by Joe Nash, Odette Phillips, Eddy Clay, John Hines, Billy Wilson, and Joan Myers Johnson. ("Ballet Hailed as One of Finest Staged By Cotillion," 1955, p. 15)

Jones attended one of Cuyjet's recitals and was impressed with her work. She was invited to choreograph and her school to perform for the cotillion on a regular basis (see Plate 10). Jones was also supportive of Sydney King and her dance studio and her advanced dancers like William Adolphus Wilson (Billy Wilson) and Joan Myers were chosen to perform and choreograph annually (M.D. Cuyjet, personal communication, November 29, 1984).

In 1954, Jones founded the Heritage House as the cultural and educational wing of the Philadelphia Cotillion Society (Doke, 1983, p. 32). By this time Black Philadelphia was in the midst of a cultural renaissance of which Jones was a prime facilitator (E.M. Dorsey, Private Collection). The Heritage House was located at Broad and Master Streets (Northcentral Philadelphia) in a mansion once owned by the nineteenth-century Shakespearean actor, Edwin Forrest (Doke,

1983, p. 32). It became a center of culture and education in Black Philadelphia and offered classes in the visual and performing arts, served as a meeting facility for several community organizations, and housed an art gallery and library (Doke, 1983, p. 33).

Jones died in 1964, yet the Heritage House continued under the directorship of Dr. John Cooper from 1964 to the early 1970s. Vera Gunn assumed the leadership position when Cooper left his post. The following excerpt describes the Heritage House:

> The founder of the society determined that there existed too few opportunities for talented youth to develop their abilities. That there was a need for an institution whereby young people could be exposed to educational and cultural outlets that were non-existent in other areas of endeavor.
>
> Today, the Heritage House has developed into a community-oriented institution; a place for general culture enrichment of community youth and adults. Here opportunities are presented for the expression of skills through training and education. The desire is to provide opportunities for children to grow, develop, and become more meaningful members of society. (Program Booklet, Philadelphia Cotillion Society Ball, Friday, December 30, 1977)

The Heritage House was discontinued in the late 1970s because of financial instability, lack of a regular staff, and a deteriorating building in need of extensive repairs. There was a campaign to revitalize it, but due to lack of community support and insufficient funding, the effort was not successful (Doke, 1983, p. 33).

Freedom Theater

Black Philadelphia became active in the national Black theater movement in the 1960s. The Philadelphia-based theater companies which predated Freedom Theater were the Afro-American Thespians, Playward Bus Company, Black Arts Spectrum Theater, and Black Butterfly (Doke, 1983, p. 33).

Freedom Theater was founded in 1966 by John Allen Jr. Allen was employed at the Sun Oil Company when he began studying acting and eventually became active in the local theater scene. Walter Palmer, a member of the Black People's Unity Movement (BPUM), invited Allen to direct a theater seminar to a group of teenagers. Allen, extremely inspired by this experience, decided to join the BPUM and established a theater unit. He left his job at Sun Oil and created Freedom Theater (Doke, 1983, p. 33).

The organization's first home was a storefront on 21st and Ridge Avenue. Using theater as a vehicle, Allen's primary objective was to bring confidence, self-identity, and discipline to urban youth. Allen decided to take theater to the people and they performed on the street, in churches, and in recreation centers. Allen was cognizant of the importance of building community support and general appreciation for theater (Wanamaker, 1985, p. 47).

Freedom Theater moved its location to the Church of the Advocate and finally secured permanent residence in the basement of Heritage House (1346 Broad Street) in 1968 and operated as a separate entity. Robert Leslie joined Allen that year and founded Freedom Theatre's Performing Arts Training Program. The institution's main thrust was to prepare young people for careers in theater while encouraging personal development and educational achievement. It offered classes in acting, voice and theater craft. Freedom Theater graduates who pursued professional careers in theater include Alfonso Alexander, Ed Bernard, Janice McClain, Richard Watson, Erika Alexander, and Samm-Art Williams (Wanamaker, 1985, pp. 48–49).

Today, Freedom Theater stages the work of major contemporary playwrights such as Douglass Turner Ward, Charles Fuller, Alice Childress, Ben Caldwell, Evan Walker, Lonnie Elder, Ed Bullins, Lorraine Hansberry, and August Wilson. It cultivates a dedicated support organization and an enthusiastic community following and eventually received substantial local, state, and federal funds to continue its mission and is nationally recognized for excellence. After the death of Allen in 1992, Dr. Walter Dallas assumed the position of Artistic Director of

Freedom Theatre and in 1993 he created a professional performing company, Freedom Repertory Theatre.

Ile Ife Black Humanitarian Center

This institution was established by the late dancer-teacher-choreographer Arthur Hall in 1969. Hall, a student of Marion Cuyjet while at the Judimar School of Dance, founded the Arthur Hall Afro-American Dance Ensemble eleven years earlier. Ile Ife provided a home for his performance ensemble and it also supported a junior company and children's company. Hall established the center as a free school of the arts that offered modern, tap, African dance, Dunham technique, Afro-Percussion, art, and language lessons in Yoruba Ige. Classes were open to children and adults, and members of the Arthur Hall Afro-American Dance Ensemble served as instructors.

Hall found a warehouse located in the 2500 block of Germantown Avenue in North Philadelphia as the site for the center and he envisioned it as a vehicle for community improvement. The Ile Ife Black Humanitarian Center became a symbol of self-help. The following is its statement of purpose:

> The Ile Ife Center exists as a means of preserving and conveying the cultural heritage of Black Americans. Mr. Hall believes that one of the basic reasons for despair and frustration within many Blacks is a sense of isolation from their past. Ile Ife's educational program helps Afro-American youth develop a sense of individual pride and confidence by reintroducing them to their rich culture and heritage. (Recital Booklet, Ile Ife Ninth Annual Recital, May 27, 1978)

In 1970, the Ile Ife center was chosen as the cultural arts program for Philadelphia's federally funded Model Cities project. The center was the beneficiary of national anti-poverty community development programs that were launched in the late 1960s (Doke, 1983, p. 35). Ile Ife received support from the National Endowment of the Arts, Pennsylvania Council of the Arts, Young Audience and Artists-in-the-Schools Programs, and Community Development

Block Grants. It offered classes year round with a summer camp for youth in North Philadelphia. The curriculum was grounded in African traditions and culture. In 1972, Hall created the Ile Ife Museum of Afro-American Culture, featuring a permanent exhibit of African and Caribbean art work (White-Dixon, 1991, p. 28).

Initially, Ile Ife received funding from local, state, and federal sources. Unfortunately, Model Cities funding ended for free classes in 1976. The center then depended on profits from the Performing Company, but financial survival was difficult and the center and museum closed in 1988.

Philadanco

The Philadelphia Dance Company (Phildanco) is a non-profit charter organization which was founded in 1970 by Joan Myers Brown. Brown, a former student of Sydney King's School of Dance, developed the dance company for the purpose of giving students at her dance school (Philadelphia School of Dance Arts) an opportunity to perform.

Although Philadanco was established to serve Brown's dance school, youth from outside the school were allowed to join. Dancers were selected by audition and they ranged in age from 14 to 25. In 1971, the school began to receive funding to support training programs for youth from underserved urban neighborhoods. The dancers received three classes daily and professional grooming in drama, make-up and costuming (Doke, 1983, p. 36). Performing outlets included churches, schools, recreation centers, and colleges.

Philadanco began to flourish in the late 1970s, but it struggled for community support. Like other arts organizations, Philadanco depends on funding from the National Endowment of the Arts, Pennsylvania Council on the Arts, and prominent Philadelphia business corporations (J.M. Brown, personal communication, September 20, 1985). Philadanco began as a community-based organization and developed into a leading professional dance company that received national acclaim (Doke, 1983, p. 37). Many of the company's former dancers have been accepted into professional companies nationwide. Several of Philadanco's dancers, including Deborah Manning, Debora Chase Hicks, David St. Charles, and the late Gary DeLoatch, continued their careers with the Alvin Ailey American Dance Theatre (Goldner, 1985, p. 1, s.L).

The State of Dance Education

During the Judimar era, there was a network of dance educators whose mission was to provide dance training for youth in Black Philadelphia. The movement to establish dance schools initially evolved because there were limited opportunities for Black youth to study dance in the larger Philadelphia community. According to dance educators Marion Cuyjet, Joan Myers Brown, and Delores Browne Abelson, many of the established dance studios in Philadelphia were closed to Blacks until the late 1950s.

This section examines dance education activity in selected privately owned dance studios. These schools served children and adults in the surrounding neighborhood as well as outside of the community and the general curriculum was ballet, jazz, tap, and acrobatics. The primary thrust was recreational and educational, rather than grooming students for professional dance careers. However, these schools nurtured the advanced dancer as well as the novice and played a vital role as a training ground for dancers, dance educators, and dance companies which emerged from the late 1950s to 1971.

For most Black children, attending a private dance school was a luxury. After World War II, Black children were more likely to attend because of slightly improved economic conditions. Children whose parents were financially unable to send them to a private dance school could receive low cost, and in some cases, free dance classes at a few city recreation centers, community arts centers, and public schools. The Wharton Center, Allens Lane Art Center, and the Settlement

Music School offered low-cost dance classes during the post-war era (J. Packman, personal communication, February 18, 1986).

Early Dance Educators

Written and oral documentation of dance educators who were active before 1926 is scant. According to Cuyjet and her contemporaries, Madame Stills, Jenny Squirrel, Lela Walker Bryant, and Essie Marie Dorsey were some of the earliest pioneers of dance education in Black Philadelphia during the late 1920s and early 1930s. Squirrel taught dance and elocution in South Philadelphia and Bryant operated a dance school in a store front in the Point Breeze section of South Philadelphia (M.D. Cuyjet, personal communication, November 29, 1984). Essie Marie Dorsey was the first teacher to provide authentic ballet technique, and she is viewed as the premier dance pioneer of dance education in Black Philadelphia (Brown, 1977, p. 12). Dancer, choreographer, and teacher, William Dollar once remarked: "Essie Marie Dorsey deserves a place in history as a pioneer spirit for the advancement of the Black dancer in American ballet" (Brown, 1977, p. 12).

Second-Generation Leaders

Marion Cuyjet and Sydney King established their dance schools during the post-World War II era. They received a positive response from the community and both schools boasted large populations. Olive Bowser, another dance educator who operated a school in West Philadelphia during the time Cuyjet and King began, was moderately successful through the 1950s (M.D. Cuyjet, personal communication, July 18,1985). In addition to Cuyjet and King, Essie Marie Dorsey and John Hines established themselves as leading dance educators in the 1950s and 1960s.

Dorsey reopened her dance studio in 1956 at her home, 239 Rittenhouse Street, in the Germantown section of Philadelphia (E.M. Dorsey, Private

Collection). She converted her living room into a dance studio. Cuyjet states: "She had a lovely large salon living room with French windows to the floor. It contained a huge ceiling to floor mirror bordered in a gold leaf frame. She had ballet barres installed in the wall" (personal communication, September 11, 1985).

Dorsey discussed her plans to open a studio with Cuyjet because she was concerned that Cuyjet and King would view a new dance studio as competition. Cuyjet assured Dorsey that they were supportive of her venture. Cuyjet comments by stating: "I told her that it would not be competition to me because we needed a school in Germantown" (personal communication, September 5, 1985).

Dorsey invited Cuyjet to teach ballet for her on Thursdays, and Cuyjet sent Dorsey a teacher for tap and jazz. Cuyjet's youngest son, Mark, three years old at the time, accompanied his mother each week. Dorsey cared for Mark while Cuyjet taught; she also provided dinner for them. Cuyjet states: "She cooked a big meal on Thursdays because she knew I would be there. She had her stepson over; so she felt like she had a family dinner. I loved those years I spent going to her school" (personal communication, September 11, 1985). Cuyjet taught for Dorsey until 1965.

Dorsey's new school was known as the Essie Marie Dance Clinic. Public relations material, which advertised Dorsey's school, highlighted the fact that she had formulated a teaching approach entitled "The Essie Marie System—A Progressive Approach" (E.M. Dorsey, Private Collection). Dorsey's pedagogy system focused on developing classical ballet bodyline, using a "hands on" teaching technique. At the core of this technique was cultivating her students' kinetic memory. Students were taken through a period in which they were only allowed to feel a particular body position before executing it. For example, Dorsey would slowly place a child's body into an arabesque position. The child would then come out of the position then assume the same position without the assistance of her teacher or the mirror (M.D. Cuyjet, personal communication, September 11, 1985).

Dorsey's school attracted children from her neighborhood, as well as those outside the community. Many of the children's parents gravitated toward Dorsey's school because of her elite social standing in the community. Dorsey taught until a few months before her death on June 8, 1967 (E.M. Dorsey, Private Collection).

Sydney Gibson King was born in Kingston, Jamaica in 1919. Her parents came to the United States as teenagers and besides King, the Gibson's had one son and another daughter. The family settled in South Philadelphia (S.G. King, personal communication, November 22, 1982). King's dancing life began in 1926 at seven years of age, and she was one of Essie Marie Dorsey's first dance students. King discusses the events surrounding her introduction to Dorsey:

> Essie Marie recruited children from the neighborhood for her school. She came around to talk to the parents. Most of the parents in that neighborhood viewed dance as "taboo." Only five mothers allowed their children to attend Essie's school. I was one of the five children and the youngest of the group. (Personal communication, November 22, 1982)

King states that her mother had a liberal attitude about exposing her children to cultural and recreational activities. She states: "Maybe it was her Episcopalian background. If we liked something, she would let us do it. We were not rich, but classes were very inexpensive. Classes were only twenty-five cents" (personal communication, February 25, 1985).

King's initial experiences at the Dorsey school were positive and she developed a preference for ballet. She was granted permission to take classes every day and eventually held the status as the school's leading dancer. Dorsey took a special interest in King and promoted her to student teacher at age twelve. King studied with Dorsey until her marriage in 1936 at age 17. Dorsey had hoped that King would pursue advanced classes, but King had no aspirations of continuing her dance studies. Her first priority was starting a family (S.G. King, personal communication, February 25, 1985).

King resumed teaching dance at the insistence of Cuyjet. Their school, the Sydney-Marion School of Dance, remained in existence for two years (1946–1948) (see Plate 11). During that time King developed a keen interest in teaching dance. She states: "I always preferred teaching. I like to see them [children] progress" (personal communication, November 22, 1982). After the Sydney-Marion School closed, King opened her own studio in the same building (711 South Broad Street). Her student population consisted of several of the children from her first school. Operating the school was a family affair. King's husband, sister, children, and extended family served as the staff (S.G. King, personal communication, November 22, 1982).

The guiding philosophy of King's school was as follows: "We are an institution dedicated to cultural, physical, and social development through the medium of dance" (Recital bulletin, Sydney School of Dance, June, 1983). The curriculum included classes in ballet, acrobatics, tap, interpretive dance (modern dance), and Dunham. King specialized in children's ballet. She hired additional teachers for tap, Dunham, and advanced ballet. Faculty members included renowned tap dancer Henry Le Tang, Arthur Hall, Eddy Clay, Dunham Technique proponent Syvilla Fort, Jerome Gaymon, Sydney's main assistant, and student teachers Billy Wilson and Joan Myers. King began to teach in Wilmington, Delaware and opened a dance school in Camden, New Jersey in the 1950s (S.G. King, personal communication, February 25, 1985).

King steered away from encouraging her students to dance professionally. She felt strongly that there was no future in dance as a career (S.G. King, personal communication, November 22, 1982). Former King students who pursued professional careers in dance are the late dancer-choreographer Billy Wilson, entertainer Lola Falana, Philadanco artistic director Joan Myers Brown, and Arthur Hall dancer Karen Steptoe Warrington.

One of Wilson's elementary school teachers, Tad Roland Johnson, encouraged his interest in dance and brought him to King's school in the 1950s. During his teen years he also studied with choreographer Antony Tudor at

Philadelphia's Ballet Guild. In the mid-1950s, Wilson performed on Broadway in *Carmen Jones and Jamaica* and he later was invited to join the Dutch National Ballet (see Plate 12). Later in his career, Wilson was acknowledged as an accomplished choreographer in a variety of dance genres. He is best known for his choreography for Broadway shows *Bubbling Brown Sugar,* the revival of *Guys and Dolls*, and staging *Eubie* during the mid-1970s. He established himself as a choreographer for modern and ballet companies and created notable dance works for Dance Theatre of Harlem *(Concerto in F)* and The Alvin Ailey American Dance Theatre (*Winter in Lisbon*) (A.W. Stripling, personal communication, February 25, 2010).

Lola Falana always wanted to dance professionally and achieved fame as a dancer-singer-actress through her work on Broadway (*Golden Boy and Dr. Jazz*), Television, Film, and as a headliner in Las Vegas. She began studying with King at age three. King vividly remembers her ambitious attitude toward performing: "Lola performed her class work like she was on stage and would always say—'Miss Sydney one day I'm goin' to make a million'" (S.G. King, personal communication, November 22, 1982). Sydney and Falana's relationship was that of a daughter and mother rather than teacher and pupil. She did not discourage Falana's aspirations to pursue a career in entertainment. Instead, she sent her to cosmetology school so she would have a vocation in addition to her dance education (S.G. King, personal communication, November 22, 1982).

Joan Myers Brown, who will be profiled later in this chapter, was King's teaching assistant, and choreographed for recitals and Christmas Cotillion performances. Karen Warrington was a student teacher, and after she left King's school she worked with the Arthur Hall Afro-American ensemble as lead dancer and publicist for ten years.

Warrington, who assumed the post as press secretary for Mayor Wilson Goode in 1985, comments on King's influence on her growth and development:

> It was important for me to have a positive outlet for my artistic interest. I believe much of what I do today is based on the love, training, and

> discipline I received through the Sydney School of dance. It was really a family. Miss Sydney was your friend, a family member. I never thought of her as a business person. She was always there for every generation. She was always doing something for her students. I don't know if she ever made any money, she was always giving it back. In traditional African and Asian cultures, in terms of a rites of passage, there are women and men who take charge of the young women and men. They help them grow, and show them what it means to be an adult. In a very real sense I think Miss Sydney was my guide, the person in charge of my age group that helped me mature. Miss Sydney reflected many of the values my parents had—she reinforced the positive values I had been taught at home. (personal communication, February 11, 1985)

In 1964, King left her studio on Broad Street and relocated to West Philadelphia (6174 Market Street) and The Sydney School of Dance continues to operate.

John Hines, born in 1925, began studying dance at the Essie Marie Dorsey School at age 11. He began with acrobatics, and eventually developed an interest in ballet, tap, and Spanish classical dance. Hines comments on the circumstances under which he began dancing: "I was very athletic. I was an avid swimmer and acrobat. I was an only child and my parents permitted me to do what I wanted" (personal communication, February 29, 1982). Hines did not experience any negative peer pressure as a result of his involvement with dance because he had established a reputation as an athlete. He was one of the few boys in attendance at the Dorsey school. Cuyjet and King, both older than Hines, were already studying with Dorsey when he arrived (J. Hines, personal communication, February 29, 1982).

Hines left the Dorsey school in 1943 at age 18 to join the army. During his army duty he performed with a male song and dance group, staged their act, and was responsible for all of the choreography (J. Hines, personal communication, February 29, 1982). That same year, Hines saw the Katherine Dunham Dance Company perform and it was a performance which made a lasting impression on him. When he left the army in 1946, he went to New York to study at the Dunham School. He enrolled in the Theatre Wing with the aid of the G.I. Bill, and studied modern dance, ballet, Dunham Technique, theatrical make-up, and percussion. Hines studied at the Dunham School daily during the summer of 1946. After he left the school, he continued his dance studies at the Ballet Arts Studio, with George Chaffe, and in Philadelphia, with Alvena Taitz, at the University of Pennsylvania (J. Hines, personal communication, February 29, 1982).

Hines introduced the Dunham technique to Philadelphia in the fall of 1946 at the Sydney-Marion School of Dance. He emerged as Philadelphia's master teacher of Dunham Technique in the 1940s. His first dance company evolved from the Sydney-Marion adult population (M.D. Cuyjet, personal communication, November 29, 1982).

When King and Cuyjet established their own schools, Cuyjet invited Hines to teach at the Judimar School of Dance. He stayed with Cuyjet until he founded his own dance school in 1959. It was located at 60th and Market and was once the dance studio of tap dancer Eleanor Harris. Hines offered ballet, tap dance, and Dunham Technique, with an emphasis on the latter. Judy Bender and George Williams comprised his core teaching staff. Hines formed a dance company with his advanced students, and its major focus was Afro-Caribbean dance forms. The company remained in existence through the early 1970s (J. Hines, personal communication, July 24, 1985).

Hines, who passed in the late-1980s, was known as a proficient ballet teacher as well as a Dunham proponent. He had a devoted student following and when he closed his school in 1961, they continued to study with him wherever he taught. He is responsible for nurturing several young men who pursued professional dance careers such as John Jones, Kevin Brown, Gary Deloatch and Robert Garland.

Third-Generation Leaders

In the 1960s and 1970s, a third generation of dance educators began to emerge. They included Joan Myers Brown, the late Arthur Hall, Ione Nash, and

Eazell Stephens. These young teachers established dance companies as well as schools. Developing a performance unit was an essential part of their mission.

Joan Myers Brown studied with Essie Marie Dorsey for a brief time as a child. She received her initial exposure to formal dance from Virginia Lingenfelder at West Philadelphia High School in the late 1940s. Brown excelled in ballet and Lingenfelder encouraged her interest, even though she knew Philadelphia's ballet community would not embrace the promising "brown ballerina" (J.M. Brown, personal communication, September 20, 1985).

Brown's mother tried to enroll her in a few white ballet schools, but she was refused admission. At age 17, Brown enrolled at the Sydney-Marion School of Dance. When King and Cuyjet dissolved their partnership Brown remained with King's school. She was promoted to assistant teacher and also assumed duties as the school's secretary. In addition, she operated King's Camden, New Jersey branch school (J.M. Brown, personal communication, September 20, 1985).

Brown met Billy Wilson at King's school and she and Wilson were two of King's most advanced students. They taught and choreographed for all the recitals and for the Annual Cotillion Society Christmas Ball. Brown strongly believes that the artistic freedom she was allowed at King's school influenced her growth and development as a teacher and choreographer (J.M. Brown, personal communication, September 20, 1985).

In the 1950s, Lingenfelder made arrangements for Brown to study with the Ballet Guild, a small company under the direction of noted dancer-choreographer Antony Tudor. Brown's performances with Ballet Guild drew controversy and even produced a bigoted response from a Philadelphia arts critic. She persevered and continued her involvement with King's school and became its leading dancer in the early 1950s (J.M. Brown, personal communication, September 20, 1985).

Brown wanted to dance professionally and Tudor advised her to leave Philadelphia in order to increase her chances for success. She secured employment as a dancer and choreographer at Club Harlem in Atlantic City in the mid-1950s and danced alongside celebrated performers such as Cab Calloway, young tap dancers Gregory and Maurice Hines, Sammy Davis Jr. and Pearl Bailey. In 1960, she decided that she wanted to stop dancing and devote her energies to teaching (see Plate 13). She opened her first school in West Philadelphia on 52nd and Walnut Streets and continued to work at Club Harlem in Atlantic City in order to finance her school (J.M. Brown, personal communication, September 20, 1985).

Cuyjet's school was beginning its second decade when Brown founded her school. Brown went to Cuyjet for advice on establishing a dance studio. Cuyjet was receptive to Brown's venture and delighted to share her expertise, just as Essie Marie Dorsey had been supportive of Cuyjet and King's efforts in that direction. Brown states:

> I went to Cuyjet for advice on opening a school. Her advice proved to be invaluable. I remember going to Cuyjet's home and sitting at her dining room table discussing the business of operating a dance school. (personal communication, September 20, 1985)

Brown established the Philadelphia School of Dance Arts with assistance from her mother and her friends. She states:

> I started the school with 30 children. They were my mother's friends children and my friends' children. Some of the parents who enrolled their children knew me from my dancing days with Sydney. Each year we got more students. (personal communication, September 20, 1985)

The school's guiding philosophy is as follows: "Our school is a place where dancers grow, where young people are given positive directives, where the community shares its potential" (J.M. Brown, Private Collection). Brown was the principal ballet teacher and she brought in teachers for modern and tap. Like her mentors, she taught the advanced dancers to teach. Brown comments by stating: "The girls that I taught at Sydney's came back and took classes with me. I gave them teaching sessions. We discussed methods and reasons for doing what we do" (personal communication, September 20, 1985).

Brown is indebted to her first teaching staff and states that she could not have survived without their assistance. They worked for small salaries and it took six years for the Philadelphia School of Dance Arts to become self-supporting. Brown left Club Harlem in 1966 so that she could dedicate herself to the development of the school. In 1970, Brown founded the Philadelphia Dance Company (Philadanco) to give her students an opportunity to perform and the company eventually gained professional status and national and international recognition (J.M. Brown, personal communication, September 20, 1985).

Arthur Hall was born in Memphis, Tennessee in 1934 and moved to Philadelphia with his mother in the early 1950s. Soon after he arrived he saw a Judimar recital. Hall states: "I moved to Philadelphia at 17 and was trying to find something to do. In Philadelphia I went to see a recital by the Judimar School. I knew this was where I could work" (Webster, 1969, p. 64). Hall studied ballet, jazz, and Dunham Technique and performed with the Judimar performance unit. His forte was Afro-Caribbean dance. Hines, Hall's Dunham instructor, took a special interest in his development. Hall later received additional classes at the Katherine Dunham School with Syvilla Fort, and studied with Lavinia Williams, Percival Borde, Walter Nicks, and Ernest L. Parham.

Hall's initial interest in choreography and concert production began at Judimar (see Plates 14 and 19). He made a special effort to observe the manner in which Cuyjet put dances together including the process of staging recitals and concerts. Hall was impressed with Cuyjet's use of a central theme in creating dance works. She was known for her story ballets and this method of presentation has influenced his choreography (A. Hall, personal communication, May 22, 1985).

In 1953, Hall met Saka Ackquye, a musician and dancer from Ghana studying for a fine arts degree at the University of Pennsylvania. Ackquye's mission was to bring African culture to Black Philadelphia. He established the

West African Cultural Society in North Philadelphia. Hall comments on Ackquye's work and his impact on him:

> He formed the West African Cultural Society and for a year went around recruiting drummers and dancers. There were 25 members. He used traditional music and sometimes wrote his own. He pulled me into African dance. It was beautiful, unique, and knowing that is important to a dancer. (Webster, 1969, p. 64)

Hall studied and performed with Ackquye for three years and in 1956 was drafted into the army. During his army duty he was assigned to Special Services as a dancer and choreographer (Webster, 1969, p. 64).

When Hall came back to Philadelphia in 1958, he began teaching at the Sydney School of Dance. He recruited dancers from the school to begin a dance company. He envisioned his own company performing African dance as a reminder to African Americans of their cultural heritage. His first repertory consisted of works recreated from Ackquye's dances (Webster, 1969, p. 64). Hall mentions the circumstances under which he formed his company:

> I used what Ackguye had built and created an American side of the thing. I was working in a badge factory all that time. When Medgar Evers was killed I stayed home a day in protest and they fired me. It made me decide to strike out on my own. My first break came when I choreographed for the Theater of the Living Arts's production of Rochelle Owen's *Belch*. (Webster, 1969, p. 64)

Hall's Afro-American Dance ensemble gained local, national, and international recognition. During their first decade the company performed for the Philadelphia Arts Festival, the Nigerian Embassy in Washington, D.C., and at Jacobs Pillow, a major summer dance festival. In the 1970s, Hall's company was selected to participate in Philadelphia's Young Audiences program (Webster, 1969, p. 65). The company also studied and performed in Ghana and Nigeria, West Africa. As noted earlier in this chapter, eleven years after he founded his dance company (1969), Hall established the Ile Ife Black Humanitarian Center, a community school of the arts in North Philadelphia, whose major focus was the preservation of African dance and culture.

Hall left Philadelphia in 1988 to reside Memphis, Tennessee and then moved to Camden, Maine in 1995. In 1994, an extensive website, The Arthur Hall Collection, was created in honor of his legacy and contributions to the arts. He continued his work as a national and international ambassador of African dance and culture until he passed in July 2000.

Ione Nash began studying dance at age 17, with Olive Bowser. She received instruction in ballet and tap and studied at the Bowser school for three years. In the mid-1950s, she left the school and enrolled at the Judimar school in order to reap the benefits of the advanced level dancing program offered by Cuyjet. Nash discovered that her level of technical proficiency was below that of dancers in her age group. She states: "Cuyjet told me that although I was considered an advanced dancer at the Bowser school that I was a beginner at Judimar. Some of my friends who came to Judimar with me quit, but I was determined to stay and catch up" (personal communication, October 4, 1985).

Nash worked diligently to become one of Judimar's most talented students and after her arrival she was selected to perform with Judimar's dance company (see Plate 14). Nash gravitated toward Afro-Caribbean and African dance forms while at the Judimar School. John Hines and Joe Nash, instructors responsible for teaching African dance forms, played an important role in Nash's development. She studied with Saka Ackquye and was one of the ten dancers chosen to be a part of his African Dance Ensemble in the early 1950s. She also formed a partnership with Arthur Hall and they performed as a duo in Philadelphia for several years (personal communication, October 4, 1985).

Nash left Judimar in the late 1950s to study at the John Hines School of Dance. During that time, she studied ballet with Thomas Cannon, Afro-Caribbean and African dance forms with Syvilla Fort and at the Olatunji School of Dance in New York City (I. Nash, personal communication, October 4, 1985). Nash's husband encouraged her to open a dance school and in 1960 she established the Ione Nash Academy of Dance. The school was located in the 5800 block of Germantown Avenue near Vernon Park. She offered courses in jazz, ballet, African, and tap to pre-teens, teens, and adults. In 1963, she formed the Ione Nash Dance Workshop, which developed into the Ione Nash Dance Company (I. Nash, personal communication, October 4, 1985). Problems developed when the community surrounding the school began to complain. Nash comments:

> We were located in a business district of Germantown. At that time the community was predominantly white. They complained that we were too noisy. They took us to court. The mothers whose children attended my school went to court and spoke in my behalf. Still we never received a license. (personal communication, October 4, 1985)

Nash's academy closed in 1964. It remained in existence for four years. She made a firm decision not to operate a school again and to teach on a free-lance basis. In the early 1970s, she rented out space at the Stephens School of Dance in Germantown's Maplewood mall, and taught dance for the Philadelphia Recreation Department. Nash's performing group continued to dance in Philadelphia and she established a reputation as one of Philadelphia's finest African and Afro-Caribbean dance instructors (M.D. Cuyjet, personal communication, November 29, 1984). Her contributions to the development of dance of the African Diaspora in Philadelphia have been documented by the Philadelphia Folklore Project.

Eazell Stephen's introduction to dance began at age eight at the Wharton recreation center with Marion Cuyjet. Her most memorable experience with Cuyjet was learning a dance piece entitled *Stormy Weather* (E.B. Stephens, personal communication, October 7, 1982).

Stephens discontinued her dance studies in high school, but in 1954 resumed her interest in college at Howard University. She majored in physical education with a concentration in dance. She received preparation in dance history, theory, composition, and modern dance technique with Martha Graham exponent Ethel

Butler, and Rona Joan Sande, a specialist in dance education and the Humphrey-Weidman system of modern dance technique (Stephens School of Dance Recital Bulletin, August 26, 1973).

Stephens returned to Philadelphia in 1959 and accepted an assignment to teach health and physical education on the secondary school level for the Philadelphia Public School System. Wherever Stephens taught, she formed a dance club and performance unit. She continued her dance studies at Temple University with Kathy Pira and at the Philadelphia Civic Ballet. In 1964, she formed the Stephens Dancers. The group performed for civic and social organization banquets, the cabaret circuit, and dinner theaters in Black Philadelphia (E.B. Stephens, personal communication, October 7, 1982).

In the late 1960s, Stephens was dance specialist for the Philadelphia recreation department's federally funded Project Renewal (Recital Bulletin, August 26, 1973). When the program was phased out, her students encouraged her to open a school of her own. Stephens opened the Stephens School of Dance, September, 1970, at 931 West Lehigh Avenue, in North Central Philadelphia. The following is a statement of the goals of the Stephens School of Dance:

> Our aims are not just to deal with our students in the areas of dance, but academically and socially as well. We are interested in the "Whole" person. Dance is just a medium of trying to reach our young people. (Stephens School of Dance Recital Bulletin, August 26, 1973)

Stephen's teaching specialization was tap dance, but she taught jazz, ballet, and modern dance. According to Stephens, the community was not receptive to ballet and modern dance technique. She states: "I lost popularity during the late 1960s because of the Black consciousness movement in North Philly" (personal communication, October 7, 1982). Stephens decided to change her teaching approach and began to offer a commercial dance technique that was a combination of jazz and modern. She left North Philadelphia in the mid-1970s to relocate to Germantown at the Maplewood mall near Greene and Maplewood

Streets. She felt that her clientele there was more receptive to a variety of dance techniques (E.B. Stephens, personal communication, October 7, 1982).

Stephens never encouraged her students to dance professionally because she strongly believed that the chances of making a viable professional dance career were extremely difficult. Instead she stressed the importance of completing high school and attending college.

The Judimar era was a time when Black Philadelphians struggled for equal rights and began to formulate their own agenda for survival by creating organizations and institutions to meet the needs of their community. The Judimar School, in addition to the dance, music, theatre, and cultural arts organizations and institutions cited in this chapter, emerged as important educational and cultural institutions that supported the social, cultural, economic, political, and educational advancement of Black Philadelphia.

The dance educators who have been highlighted in this chapter were leading proponents of dance education in Black Philadelphia during the Judimar era, 1948 to 1971. Essie Marie Dorsey initiated the movement to provide quality dance preparation for youth in Black Philadelphia, and her former students Cuyjet, King, and Hines, perpetuated her legacy. Consequently, these educators nurtured Brown, Hall, Nash, and Stephens, a third generation of dance educators whose work had an immense impact on dance education in Black Philadelphia during and after the Judimar era. For the purpose of this study, this significant period in the history of the Black Philadelphia community is termed "the Judimar era." The next chapter focuses on the Judimar School.

CHAPTER 4

Judimar School of Dance (1948–1971)

Historical Background

Cuyjet established the Judimar School of Dance in 1948. Her primary motivation for continuing to operate a dance school after she dissolved her partnership with King was to provide opportunities in training and performance for youth in Black Philadelphia. There were very few dance schools in Black Philadelphia, and many of the established dance schools in the larger Philadelphia community would not admit Black students (M.D. Cuyjet, personal communication, November 29, 1984).

Cuyjet created the title of the school by combining her daughter's name with her own (Judith/Marion). Judimar was located in the commercial business district of Center City Philadelphia. Cuyjet viewed Philadelphia's downtown area as a prime location. She states:

> Center city was centrally located. We could pull students from all over Philadelphia and the tri-state area. The area was pleasant and considered the hub of the arts scene in Philadelphia. Students could come on public transportation. Their parents did not have to worry about parking. Having a dance school in center city was new for us, a phenomenon for Black families. (personal communication, February 13, 1986)

During the emergence of Judimar, Cuyjet's initial vision was to be responsible for nurturing the first Black ballerina to attain professional status. Cuyjet states:

> My goal was to make the first Black ballerina on pointe, in New York, performing in a meaningful situation. It may not have been with a company. Janet Collins got there first at age 38, dancing with the New York Metropolitan Opera. I was happy that she got there. (personal communication, November 29, 1984)

In the early 1950s, Cuyjet's goal began to shift. She states:

> Then, I wanted to make as many ballerinas as possible, but they had to be brown-skinned. They had to look Negro. We were not calling ourselves Black back then. If she could pass for white, forget it. That would not give me anything. Her picture had to tell the whole story. I never worried about the light-skinned girls. It was the brown-skinned girls I had to open doors for. (personal communication, February 13, 1986)

Cuyjet's major objective was twofold: first, to make dancers, and second, to provide dance preparation to all youth as a vehicle for social, cultural, intellectual, and physical development. The latter aspect of her objective may have been influenced by the general dissemination of John Dewey's theory of progressive education which was gaining impetus in public school education in the 1950s. This educational theory supports the total development of the child.

The following statement of aim is from two Judimar School of Dance recital bulletins:

> The broad aim of Judimar is that it is a laboratory for social as well as artistic development in the formation of well integrated personalities. (Judimar School, Recital Bulletin, June, 1950)

> The student is encouraged to use initiative to develop the traits of character which will be required for success and mastery of technique that is essential to the creation of the important dancers of tomorrow. (Judimar School, Recital Bulletin, June, 1954)

Although Cuyjet aspired to nurture her dancers toward professional status, she never suggested that they pursue dancing careers. Instead, she provided training experiences that would enable them to realize their full potential.

According to Judith Jamison, Elmer Ball, and Donna Lowe Warren, former students, Cuyjet never verbally encouraged them to dance professionally. Judith Jamison states that she only encouraged them to do their best (personal communication, May 15, 1985). It is clear that Cuyjet was a pragmatist and a realist. Her dance education philosophy was shaped not only by her desire to train "well-integrated personalities," but also by her knowledge of the limitations that existed for Black careers in dance due to racial discrimination.

Cuyjet and her husband Stephen encouraged all of their students to receive a college education. She comments on her attitude toward higher education:

> Both my husband and I were very oriented to college. We encouraged all the students to attend college. In fact that is what they worked toward. They and we knew that when they graduated from high school, they were going to college. Whatever their major was going to be, we wanted them to do that first. We talked about having to fit dance into that, if they cared to. There was the option of majoring in dance, but only a few schools offered ballet majors, and those were not kindly to Blacks. (personal communication, February 13, 1986)

Former students attribute Judimar's success to Cuyjet's undaunted spirit, positive attitude, and ambitious disposition. Delores Browne Abelson comments on her earliest impression of Cuyjet:

> Marion was in her mid-twenties when she began her school. She was a mother of two small children at the time. She was energetic and ambitious. I was impressed with her sophistication, energy, and dedication to the craft. (personal communication, August 23, 1985)

Cuyjet's spirited attitude influenced the school's atmosphere. Joe Nash, a former faculty member, states:

> I had never met a woman whose enthusiasm was so contagious. When Marion took hold of an idea she saw it through from beginning to end. Her energy was extraordinary. It caused the whole school to move with zest and excitement. (personal communication, August 16, 1985)

According to former students, interpersonal relationships among students were positive, and if a dispute occurred, Stephen Cuyjet settled the disagreement. Many students refer to Judimar as one big family. There was a strong sense of community. Stephen Cuyjet, Jr., comments on the school's atmosphere: "The school was very family-ish. 'Miss Marion' and 'Mr. Steve' were almost surrogate parents for some of the children" (personal communication, March 1, 1986).

Cuyjet's daughter states that Judimar possessed both an academic and domestic atmosphere:

> Students came directly from school. All of us did our homework there. Judimar was a homey set up. It was a home away from home. Wherever the school was located mother would arrange to have cooking facilities. She would cook one-pot meals. Father came to school after work. He was the "provost marshall." (personal communication, September 7, 1985)

Judimar was, indeed, a family affair. Cuyjet and her husband co-directed the school, and their three children took dance classes at the school. She comments on the family involvement in a 1974 *Philadelphia Inquirer* article: "Stephen and I were in business together. He handled the business end. All three children, Mark, Judy, and Stephen, Jr., had to attend dancing school almost every day so I could see them" (M.D. Cuyjet, Private Collection).

Cuyjet's oldest son, Stephen, was more directly involved with the behind-the-scenes operation of Judimar than Mark and Judy. He served as the school's custodian from 1954 until 1958, and by the time he was in high school and college, he assumed recital production responsibilities. Stephen Cuyjet, Jr. reminisces about the circumstances under which he became involved with recital production:

> In high school, I shared time with my mother during the night time. She was a late night worker. She would sit at the dining room table sketching costumes and dances on paper. The house was quiet. That is when she could work. She started bouncing ideas off me. I slowly became involved with the production aspect of the business and the

> shows. By eleventh grade I got in production, and in college I helped as a back stage monitor. (personal communication, March 1, 1986)

The support system provided by Cuyjet's parents enabled her to balance career and family successfully (see Plate 15). Judy Cuyjet comments on her maternal grandmother's role during the development of Judimar:

> My grandmother was the woman of the house and we respected that. She was the authority figure. She raised the children, bought our clothes, and so on. My mother was a housewife in the summer, but my grandmother still ran the house. My grandparents gave up their apartment to live with us so they could raise us. They did this so mother could be free to run her school, (personal communication, September 7, 1985)

Judimar had six different locations. The first was 1310 Walnut Street, third floor. The owner of the building was white. According to Cuyjet, when he visited the school one Saturday he was surprised to discover that the children were Black. Cuyjet comments: "If you are going to pioneer [something] don't tell them what you are going to do" (personal communication, November 29, 1984). Nothing resulted from the proprietor's discovery. Cuyjet remained at her first location for two years, 1948 to 1950. She moved the school to a new location because the space would not accommodate the growing student population. When Cuyjet rented her studio, the landlord assumed that she was white; she "passed" not by lying, but by going along with his assumption. The fact that he allowed her to stay meant that some small inroad had been made for African Americans to be able to rent studios in Center City.

In 1950, Cuyjet moved the school to 1227 Walnut Street. The studio was located on the second floor above a restaurant. During the latter part of their first year in residence, the owner asked them to move because of noise. Cuyjet was in the midst of mounting *Carmen* for their recital. Her lawyer, William Coleman, contested their request. After negotiations they reluctantly granted her a lease for another year. During the second year, the owners were persistent with their request for Cuyjet to vacate the premises and they agreed to pay her moving expenses.

Cuyjet moved a third time. The new studio, located at 1215 Walnut Street, was about five doors away from her previous address. She remained in this studio from 1952 to 1954. During this period she became pregnant with her third child, Mark.

Cuyjet again encountered difficulty with the landlord. He complained that the students were too noisy. The method used to encourage Cuyjet to move involved a fire escape violation. The fire department issued an ultimatum which stated the school would have to vacate the premises unless their fire escape was repaired. The landlord promised to attend to the problem, yet he never made the necessary adjustments. Cuyjet moved in 1954.

Judimar's fourth studio was located 1618 North Broad Street, over a record shop. The school was in operation less than a year before the owner asked that she leave because of the noise. He made and kept his commitment to assist with the move.

Cuyjet speculates that the reason she had so much difficulty in securing a permanent space for the school in the commercial business district of Center City was that the school was Black. She states: "They asked me to move because of the noise. But I think the kids were too visible. They used the noise factor instead of race to avoid a discrimination suit from the Urban League or the National Association for the Advancement of Colored People" (personal communication, November 29, 1984). Cuyjet was attempting to integrate an all-white Center City business district during an era when civil rights litigation to achieve equal rights for Black Americans was becoming frequent.

In the fall of 1954, the school moved to its fifth location, 2011 Chancellor Street. This was her last studio downtown. Cuyjet rented the entire building and named it "The Dance Educators Building." The school was a cooperative venture with two other dance schools. They were The John Hines School of Theatre Arts and The Anne Bernadino School of Tap. The director of each school also taught for Cuyjet. Recitals included all three schools. The following program note explains the Dance Educators' concept:

> In September, 1954, Judimar joined forces with dance teachers specializing in other fields of dance, who wished to establish themselves as separate schools of dance. Each of these teachers are firm in their belief that a student should have a teacher-specialist for each dance subject. The end result of such a system enables the dancer to respect each phase as an outstanding art. (Judimar Recital Bulletin, June 17, 1955)

Cuyjet remained at her fifth location for five years. In 1958, she decided to discontinue operating a school. Stephen Cuyjet had become ill with Huntington's Disease, a genetic brain disorder. She decided that a full-time teaching schedule would not allow adequate time to care for her husband. She rented space at the Jay Dash Studios on 13th Street between Sansom and Walnut Streets and taught ballet and jazz on Thursdays and Fridays (personal communication, November 29, 1984).

The Cuyjet family had just moved to Southwest Philadelphia, 944 South 58th Street. In addition to her classes at the Dash studio, she began to offer classes in the basement of their new home. In the fall of 1958, Cuyjet decided to reopen Judimar full time. It was imperative that she find a studio in the vicinity of her home so she could be close to her husband. She found a two-story building across the street from her house at 1014 South 58th Street. This was Judimar's final location (M.D. Cuyjet, personal communication, November 29, 1984).

By 1958, Cuyjet had begun to establish branch schools. They were as follows: Germantown Branch, 239 Rittenshouse Street (Dorsey's home); Center City Branch, J. Dash Studios; and Princes Anne Maryland Branch, Maryland State College. Cuyjet maintained a part time teaching schedule at each branch (E.M. Dorsey, Private Collection).

Although the main Judimar school relocated several times during the 1950s, its transient nature did not affect student enrollment. "Each time she moved, the students moved with her" (J. Jamison, Lecture/Performance, February 10, 1985).

Throughout its existence, Judimar remained one of the most popular dance schools in Black Philadelphia.

According to Cuyjet's family and colleagues, Judimar was in its heyday during the 1950s. Its popularity was fueled by Black Philadelphia's cultural renaissance, spearheaded by Eugene W. Jones, and by the success of Black dancers on the New York dance scene. In the 1950s, they were becoming a part of the mainstream concert and Broadway dance culture (Jackson, 1966, pp. 19–20). Young dancers like Alvin Ailey, Mary Hinkson (a native Philadelphian), Carmen de Lavallade, Arthur Mitchell, and Judimar dancers Delores Browne Abelson and John Jones, were among New York's most gifted dance artists.

Cuyjet's daughter refers to the 1960s as the beginning of the end for Judimar School of Dance. The enrollment had decreased to around 100 because of the competition created by dance studios established by the third-generation dance proponents. Cuyjet's family obligations, faltering health, and exhausting teaching schedule made it increasingly difficult to continue to operate the school.

In the early 1950s, Cuyjet sustained a serious fall down the cellar steps at her home in Southwest Philadelphia. That accident initiated a spinal problem that plagued her throughout the Judimar era. The injury was complicated by a car accident in 1954 and stress incurred through lifting dancers in partnering class. Cuyjet's spinal condition deteriorated in the late 1960s and she underwent surgery in 1968 (M.D. Cuyjet, personal communication, February 13, 1986). After surgery she decided to discontinue the school. She states:

> I had to close my school. I couldn't teach all those classes. During the time I had my spinal surgery, and couldn't teach, I had to pay a substitute to teach my classes. It cost me three times my allotted salary to pay Sylvia Kimmelman, a local ballet dancer, to teach. (personal communication, February 13, 1986)

The Judimar School of Dance closed in 1971.

Organizational Structure

Cuyjet's colleagues and former students often remark that Judimar was one of the few professionally operated private dance schools in Philadelphia. John Hines states that the school was the first private dance studio run as a professional ballet school and that it was patterned after established ballet schools where Cuyjet had studied (personal communication, July 24, 1985).

The following section examines the school's organizational structure.

Curriculum

Judimar's most unique feature was that its emphasis was ballet. Very few Black dance schools during this era, with the exception of the Sydney School of Dance, and the Jones-Haywood School in Washington, D.C., specialized in ballet. Cuyjet strongly believed that ballet was an essential technique. She states:

> No matter what type of dancer you are going to be, you are never going to be up to your full capacity unless you also study ballet. You don't have to perform classical ballet, but ballet is going to refine a lot of your work so that you can be versatile. (personal communication, February 13, 1986)

Although the school's focus was ballet, students were required to take other dance techniques. Cuyjet had the desire to develop versatile dancers. Joe Nash, former Judimar instructor, praises Cuyjet's interest in nurturing well-rounded dancers:

> They [the students] were so flexible. Those students were amazing. They could move from one dance style to the other. That was valuable training they received with Marion. I applaud her for what she did, she prepared them to be ballet dancers or modern. The students were introduced to the full spectrum of dance. (personal communication, August 23, 1985)

Judimar offered classes in the following courses: ballet (pointe included), partnering, "Primitive" (a term used at Judimar to denote a combination of African and Afro-Caribbean dance forms), interpretive (a term used at Judimar to denote a combination of Afro-Caribbean dance forms and modern dance technique), tap, jazz, acrobatics, social dance, folk dance, and children's dance (M.D. Cuyjet, Private Collection).

In 1949, Judimar initiated an adult class. The following excerpt from a Judimar recital bulletin describes its emphasis:

> One of the newer innovations at JUDIMAR is the Adult class, both beginning and advanced, in modern and interpretive dance, perhaps the most interesting of all. [sic]
>
> Here is the aura of informality, spiked with humor and the ability to laugh at oneself, the once-timid adult, under patient guidance and direction, learns first the simpler exercises and techniques. The beginner is there for many reasons: for some it is a continuation of training, for others a brand new experience. Many join to lose weight or condition the body, while others are there for the pure joy of dancing.
>
> Those who take a more serious interest in the dance as an art form "graduate" into the advanced class. There one learns to combine the single and isolated techniques learned into a more complex dance pattern.
>
> The classes are under the capable direction of instructor John Hines, known to many as the leading exponent in Philadelphia of the famed Dunham Technique. (Judimar School, Recital Bulletin, June, 1950)

In 1950, the school initiated classes in "Primitive" dance for children. The following excerpt is taken from a 1950 *Philadelphia Tribune* article entitled "Judimar School of Dance Endorses Course in Primitive for Youngsters.":

> The Judimar School of Dance, 1227 Walnut Street, is offering the best qualified teachers for instruction of students in dance. Mrs. Marion Cuyjet, director of the school, has announced the retention to her teaching staff John Hines, one of the nation's most outstanding exponents of Dunham Technique.
>
> This year Hines will add a children's course in primitive dance and percussion to his interpretive curricula. This course in primitive will be of interest to small boys whose parents desire them to pursue the field of dance under efficient instruction. (M.D. Cuyjet, Private Collection)

The school operated Monday through Saturday and the majority of classes were offered on Saturdays. Classes began weekdays at 3:30 and early morning on the weekend. In the early 1950s, an exercise class for housewives was held in the early afternoon during the week. The daily class schedule ran until 10 p.m. The Cuyjet family left the studio each night at 11:00 p.m. (J. Colvin, personal communication, September 7, 1985).

Students generally took two classes a week. The advanced dancers came to the school three to five times a week, and averaged six classes a week. Cuyjet assigned the classes they were to take (S. Cuyjet, personal communication, March 1, 1986). Levels of instruction included beginning, intermediate, and advanced. Students were placed according to age and ability. Advanced students were placed in special pre-professional classes (J. Hines, personal communication, July 24, 1985).

Primitive dance was popular at the Judimar School from 1949 to the mid-1950s, due to the success of the Dunham Technique and the Cuban musical and dance craze. Hines, the director for this course, left Judimar in 1960, and classes were discontinued. Jazz dance replaced it in popularity emerging as a popular American dance technique in the late 1950s. Cuyjet took advantage of its popularity and began to offer Luigi-style jazz classes in 1956. Cuyjet held special classes in partnering (male, female duet work in ballet), for the advanced dancers because regular classes did not provide adequate time. Cuyjet states: "We had special Sunday partnering sessions. Camaradarie was great! Students enjoyed partnering" (personal communication, April 3, 1986).

Cuyjet supplemented the curriculum with special seminars and master classes taught by guest teachers. In the early 1950s, she invited Joe Nash to give a lecture demonstration on his work in professional concert and Broadway dance (see Plate 16) (J. Nash, personal communication, August 16, 1985). December 1965, Cuyjet invited teacher, choreographer, Joan Kerr, to teach a master class in Horton Technique (G. Celain, Private Collection).

Judimar sponsored a few six-week summer dance camps in the 1950s and 1960s. The program was geared toward the advanced dancer. Classes offered included ballet, pointe, acrobatics, jazz, tap, folk, percussion (drumming), and modern dance. "The summer dance camp was for the better dancers. They took three classes a day, studied with a guest teacher, and took cultural trips to the museum or the like so they could expand their artistic interest beyond dance" (J. Colvin, personal communication, September 7, 1985). (see Appendix C for tuition rates.)

Cuyjet constantly sought enrichment experiences for her students. As mentioned in Chapter Two, she took her advanced dancers to New York City to study. She took as many as 24 girls, ages six to twelve, to study during the winter, the spring, and during Christmas vacation. For overnight trips they stayed at the Tatum House of the YWCA on Lexington Avenue at 38th Street.

The following photograph caption is from an un-credited newspaper clipping which publicized one of Judimar's New York trips:

> "Gave Vacations to Their Art." Students who went to New York and completed a summer course at Ballet Arts, Carnegie Hall. Posing at the barre are Frances Jimenez, Juanita Jones, Delores Browne, Gloria Higdon, and Judy Cuyjet. (M.D. Cuyjet, Private Collection)

Delores Browne Abelson comments on her New York dance experiences:

> She [Cuyjet] drove us to New York and registered us in schools. We went to the Dunham school; we went to Ballet Arts. We had partnering, pointe, and folk dance. Dunham was a wonderful experience. When we went we were already advanced level, and we were just kids. That was quite an experience for us. Cuyjet also took classes. We brought back the skills we had. We would then work with the other kids with what we had gained. (personal communication, August 23, 1985)

Cuyjet seized any opportunity to provide advanced dance preparation for her students. This unwavering commitment distinguished her among dance educators in Black Philadelphia as well as in the larger dance education community.

Faculty

From 1950 to 1958, Cuyjet's core teaching faculty consisted of John Hines and Anne Bernadino Hughes. She met both colleagues as a student at the Essie Marie Dorsey school.

Hines taught ballet, tap, Interpretive, and Afro-Caribbean (Dunham) dance forms. He also coordinated the adult and primitive dance division. During the mid-1950s, he became involved with the professional dance arena and performed in a summer stock production of *Showboat*, at Jones Beach, Long Island, New York. In addition, he performed with the Walter Nicks Dance Company in Havana, Cuba for three months (Judimar School Recital Bulletin, June, 1955). His background experience in costuming, theatrical makeup, and Caribbean drumming proved to be an asset during the Judimar recital season.

Hughes was in charge of tap classes. She studied ballet with Tom Cannon and Essie Marie Dorsey, tap with Jack Stanley, and jazz and boogie with Charlie Morrison in New York City. In the late 1930s and early 1940s, she choreographed for Philadelphia's National Youth Administration productions. Hughes was director of the school's tap department until 1955. At that time she opened her own school in Cuyjet's Dance Educators Building. She taught part time for Cuyjet until 1958 (Judimar School, Recital Bulletin, June 17, 1955).

Frances (Franca) Jimenez, Gladys Snyder, Terez Nelson, Shirley Elsey, and Betty Lewis, composed Judimar's first support faculty (see Plate 17). Jimenez taught ballet and she studied with Cuyjet and Cannon until 1957 (see Plate 18). That year, she joined the New York Negro Ballet Company (Ballet Americana) and toured Great Britain then performed in Europe for two years (M.D. Cuyjet, personal communication, November 29, 1984).

Cuyjet began to attract a large number of male students in the early 1950s, and she felt that it was important to expand her male faculty. She brought New York dancers Joe Nash and Ernest Leigh Parham to Judimar during that time. Cuyjet met Parham when he came to Philadelphia with the Dunham Company in the late 1940s. His specialization was Dunham Technique and modern dance. He left New York to teach and choreograph in Philadelphia in the early 1950s. Parham worked primarily with Judimar's advanced dancers.

In addition to teaching courses in Dunham and modern, he choreographed for Judimar's experimental choreography workshop (Judimar School, Recital Bulletin, June 18, 1954). The pieces which evolved out of the workshop were designed to showcase the advanced dancers' technical proficiency. Parham left the school in 1953 in order to join the Dunham Company for their Australian tour (see Plate 19). He later performed with the Alvin Ailey American Dance Theatre during its emergence in the late 1950s (J. Nash, personal communication, August 16, 1985).

Joe Nash (Joseph Vincent Nash) replaced Parham. He comments on the circumstances under which he began to teach at Judimar:

> One of Cuyjet's publicity agents, Eddie Gaines, asked me to come to Philly to teach at Judimar. I welcomed the opportunity immediately. Ernie Parham was about to leave, and they needed somebody to take his place. I was impressed with her [Cuyjet] immediately. She took me in as if we had been old friends. (personal communication, August 16, 1985)

Nash had been dancing professionally since 1945. His career began with Afro-Caribbean dance pioneer, Beryl McBurnie (Belle Rosette). After leaving her company in 1946, he performed in several Broadway musicals including *Showboat* and *Finian's Rainbow*. He was lead dancer with the Pearl Primus Dance Company and the Donald McKayle Dance Company in the late 1940s and early 1950s. Nash made a special appearance with the Charles Weidman Dance Theatre and danced under the direction of choreographers Helen Tamiris, Michael Kidd, Valerie Bettis and Hanya Holm (Judimar School, Recital Bulletin, June 17, 1955).

During his *Showboat* experience he began collecting and documenting Afro-American dance. Nash, who passed in 2005, was the leading authority on 20th century Black Concert Dance in the United States. His private collection is housed at the Schomburg Center for Research in Black Culture.

Nash taught ballet, modern, and jazz at Judimar. Like Parham, he taught and choreographed for the advanced students. In the summer of 1954, he taught a special one-week seminar for professional-level dancers. Nash reflects on his early impressions of the Judimar dancers:

> When I arrived in July 1953, Cuyjet suggested that I give a seminar to introduce people to me. I presented a lecture-demonstration with the children and the professional group. I discussed my experiences in theater. The whole idea was to introduce students to the world of dance through my background. It worked beautifully. When I began working for Cuyjet, she said: "Joe, wait until you see some of the students I want you to teach." She wanted to see if I agreed with her about their potential. First I noticed John Jones, an elegant dancer, then I saw Delores Browne at the barre, and said to myself, this is my ballerina. Judy Jamison was a little girl at the time. Nobody thought she would develop into the ultimate dance star. (personal communication, August 16, 1985)

Nash briefly discusses his indebtedness to Cuyjet and the role that Judimar played in his professional growth and development.

> I am forever grateful to her. She helped me explore these talents of mine, which I would have never had the opportunity in New York City, as a choreographer with the recitals and the cotillion, a major T.V. show (Dave Garroway *Today* show), and for an opera (*Aida*, for the National Negro Opera Company). All of these went on my credits. Marion provided me the opportunity to explore a side of my background that I just did not know I had. I was refining my choreography and teaching skills and learning how to relate to people. As you know, in the world of dance you can be so caught up in pursuing your own career that you are inclined to be self-centered. But it is very important to be able to relate to people, to sense their needs, and how to encourage people who have the potential for greatness. How to help people discover themselves in a sense, that's what we were doing. We were giving those kids the opportunity to take a good hard look at themselves, to understand that the dancer's life is short and highly competitive, therefore you've got to be darn good. You cannot be haphazard and lackadaisical about your career, you've got to be serious. (personal communication, August 16, 1985)

Cuyjet felt that it was important to provide her students with the opportunity to study with dancers from New York. Nash states that she wanted to expose the students to dance personalities from the New York dance scene so that they could become familiar with the most recent trends in Broadway and concert dance (personal communication, August 16, 1985).

Cuyjet frequently invited guest teachers to Judimar. They included George Chaffee, Thomas Cannon, and Antony Tudor. During the period that intermediate and advanced students studied with guest ballet teachers, they were also required to study with Cuyjet (M.D. Cuyjet, personal communication, February 13, 1986).

According to Cuyjet's former students, she did not hoard her dancers. When she thought they could benefit from additional dance preparation outside of Judimar, she encouraged them to go. Donna Lowe Warren states:

> Mrs. Cuyjet encouraged us to take classes with famous teachers. She would not hold us back and make us study with her. We learned from everybody. She instilled in us that she wasn't the only one who could teach us. (personal communication, September 28, 1985)

In the 1950s, Cuyjet suggested that her advanced students attend West Philadelphia High School because of their excellent ballet program under the direction of Virginia Lingenfelder.

Former students are amazed at Cuyjet's ability to "share" her students with the larger dance community. Even though they studied with renowned teachers and left the fold occasionally, their respect for Cuyjet's teaching skills remained constant (D.B. Abelson, personal communication, August 23, 1985). Although Cuyjet was a realist, she was also a woman with a vision—the vision of producing Black ballerinas. Thus, the need to hold onto her students in order to insure enrollment at Judimar was tempered by her desire to send her advanced students on to opportunities that might allow them entry into the professional white ballet world.

Cuyjet's faculty diminished when she relocated to Judimar's final studio in West Philadelphia in 1958. Most of her original teaching faculty had established schools of their own or taught elsewhere. From 1958 to the late 1960s, Barbara Bullock, a former student, was the only core teacher besides Cuyjet. Bullock taught jazz. The support faculty included Tommy Jordan (jazz) and Carol Shepard (ballet). From 1969 to 1971, Judimar advanced dancers Rodney Green, Tawny Turner, and Mark Cuyjet were senior teachers.

Throughout the school's existence Cuyjet used student teachers. Five were assigned each school year. They were usually the advanced students. She guided their development just as Dorsey had done for her. She observed while they taught, and some of them eventually graduated to the status of apprentice teachers and senior teachers. Past student teachers include Rodney Green, Tawny Turner, Sally Anne Richardson, Elmer Ball, Donna Lowe Warren, Judith Jamison, Delores Browne Abelson, Tina Johnson, and Gwendolyn Peterson. Apprentice teachers included Rita Cottman, Benita Bryan, Kim Johnson, Janice Lindsay, Michele Treherne, and Mingnon Treherne (Judimar Recital Bulletins, 1950, 1954, 1955, 1962, 1966, 1970).

Warren comments on her student teaching experience: "It was one of the scariest things. She watched us teach. We learned by watching her. She gave constructive criticism after class" (personal communication, September, 28, 1985). Abelson reminisces:

> She always would oversee whoever practice-taught the classes. One wonderful thing I look back on: we were always paid. It was not much but she said, "if you are working you should be paid." That was the late 1940s and early 1950s. We were just kids, (personal communication, August 23, 1985)

The manner in which Cuyjet trained her students to teach was based on the way she had been nurtured by Essie Marie Dorsey. She carried these basic teaching premises with her throughout her career.

Students

Judimar's initial population consisted of children who had studied with Cuyjet at the Sydney-Marion School of Dance (see Plate 20). Finding students was not problematic for Cuyjet. "When I started, I did not worry about getting students. You got students from your contemporaries, from your social life" (M.D. Cuyjet, personal communication, July 18, 1985). She decided to recruit children whom she considered promising students. She went back to Barratt, her former junior high school, in order to choose her first group of scholarship students. Returning to the school was a significant occasion. Cuyjet comments:

> I went back to Barratt because there was a teacher (Virginia Lingenfelder) I wanted to show something to. She ate a lot of "crow" but nicely. She gave me praise for my endeavors. I told her, "You wouldn't let me in that ballet club, but I brought myself back here to offer two scholarships." Lingenfelder said that she did not choose me because I was too tall and lanky, and did not have enough potential, that I moved in six different directions, that I needed a lot of work to bring it together. She said she did not want me to mess up her ballets. (personal communication, November 29, 1984)

Cuyjet chose Alice Mays and Juanita Jones as scholarship recipients (see Plates 21 and 22). She had seen them dance previously at a YMCA function. Lingenfelder asked her to take another student, Sadie Delores Browne, a close friend of Mays and Jones. Cuyjet hesitated because she had never seen her dance before, but decided to grant her a scholarship. Cuyjet continued to donate two scholarships to Barratt annually (personal communication, November 29, 1984).

Cuyjet recruited on a moderate level and there were frequent articles and advertisements in the Black Press. Judimar was publicized in the *Philadelphia Tribune*, the *Philadelphia Independent*, Philadelphia editions of the *Pittsburgh Courier, and Afro-American* and *Color Magazine*. Essie Marie Dorsey assisted with recruitment on a small scale and she frequently included Judimar announcements on her dance clinic flyers (E.M. Dorsey, Private Collection).

Judimar's student enrollment stabilized at 200 in the early 1950s. The student population consisted of children (preschool through teens) and adults. Many of the adults had had previous dance experience and were attracted to the school because of the Primitive and interpretive (modern dance) classes.

Judimar was predominately Black. The white students in attendance were adult dancers who enrolled for Dunham technique. During the early 1950s, Judimar was advertised as an interracial school. An uncredited newspaper clipping from Cuyjet's private collection reads: "Interracial Dance School Notes Record Enrollment." Another clipping bills Judimar as "The Unusual Interracial School" (M.D. Cuyjet, Private Collection).

The following program note is a concise rationale for the establishment of Judimar and states its interracial policy.

> The Judimar School of Dance was founded by its director Marion D. Cuyjet, who recognized the importance of a school where Negroes interested in ballet, modern, and related forms of instruction could receive training and have the opportunity to display these talents to their best advantage. Although this need was the moving force in establishing JUDIMAR, the school is interracial in nature and welcomes all peoples and all groups who adhere to the creed of brotherhood. (Judimar School, Recital Bulletin, June n.d., 1950)

Judimar served children from various backgrounds. According to Cuyjet, a large percentage of the children's parents were school teachers. During that era these families were considered middle class in the Black community. There were also children who were members of Jack and Jill, Inc., a national, family oriented, service foundation and social club for middle-class Blacks (S. Cuyjet, personal communication, March 1, 1986). Cuyjet's daughter states that it was difficult to decipher what type of economic background the children were from. "I assume most were from working-class families. No one came to school tattered or unable to pay for classes. The talented students who could not afford to pay for classes were put on scholarship" (J. Colvin, personal communication, September 7, 1985).

In the early to late 1950s, Cuyjet had to contend with parents who wanted separate classes for their children based on their middle-class status. Most of them were doctors, lawyers, journalists, or school teachers. Cuyjet states that blatant elitism was prevalent during that era. "There were about six girls whose parents requested separate classes. They offered to pay more for classes. This situation existed seven or eight years during the 1950s" (M.D. Cuyjet, November 29, 1984).

Judimar primarily served two types of students. There were children who came for recreational, educational, and cultural enrichment, and there were the "dancers," the advanced students who quietly aspired to dance professionally. Many of them received full scholarships. They had specific responsibilities: cleaning the studios, answering phones, and running errands. Scholarship students took at least two classes a day (J. Colvin, personal communication, September 7, 1985). Stephen Cuyjet, Jr. believes that his mother's practice of granting scholarships to talented students evolved from her experiences with Dorsey. "Mother could not afford classes and Aunt Essie put her on scholarship. I believe this influenced my mother. 'If a student wants to dance, make a way for them.' That was the atmosphere" (personal communication, March 1, 1986).

In 1950, Judimar established a scholarship fund for advanced dancers. The following statement of purpose appeared in Judimar's recital bulletin:

> This year witnesses the establishment of a Scholarship Fund for the purpose of providing the many pairs of ballet shoes, costumes, and other expenses for those unable to meet financial requirements, for those who possess distinctive talent and ability, with the promise of becoming truly great dancers. It is hoped that the public will respond generously and encourage artistic youth. (Judimar Recital Bulletin, n.m., 1950)

Judimar was fortunate to have a large number of male students during the 1950s. (In past and present eras males have traditionally been a minority population in the field of dance.) Most of them were on scholarship. Young men who studied at the school during this era included: George Williams, Ronald

Platts, Melvin Brooms, Elmer Ball, McCoy Tyner, Samuel Caruthers, Garvin Masseaux, Charles Medley, Charles Moore (not to be confused with the dancer who performed with the Dunham Company), and George Waters (Judimar School Recital Bulletin, June 18, 1954). Cuyjet began with a small number of male dancers in the early 1950s and eventually these dancers recruited others (see Plate 19). Ball states:

> Cuyjet used the guys to recruit others. The atmosphere was highly competitive. The male dance teachers from New York (Nash and Parham) taught us to project a masculine image on stage. Portions of most classes were devoted to the men. (personal communication, September 4, 1985)

The following excerpt is taken from a newspaper article publicizing a Judimar male scholarship audition:

> Marion Cuyjet has studied Russian, French and Italian styles of ballet. The present enrollment is 200. This year the school will offer several male scholarships. Judimar is now rated one of Philadelphia's foremost dance schools for Negroes. [pictured are George Morgan, Duran Johnson, Dorrie Holden, Wesley Brown, John Jones, and Francis Portlock] ("Judimar 1215 Walnut, Offers Male Scholarships," September 1, 1951)

Soon after this article, a picture of the young men who won scholarships appeared in the *Philadelphia Tribune*. The caption read: "Win Scholarships to Dance School." John Jones, who later pursued a professional dance career, was among the seven scholarship recipients (M.D. Cuyjet, Private Collection) (see Plate 23).

Judimar boasted an array of female as well as male advanced dancers. Every few years, a group of young women would emerge as school "stars." Cuyjet refers to periods in Judimar's development according to the female dancers who were the most accomplished at the time. Judimar's first era, 1948 to 1953, was marked by a group of dancers Cuyjet refers to as the "big three," Delores Browne Abelson, Alice Mays, and Juanita Jones (see Plate 24). Judy Cuyjet (see Plate 25), Gloria Higdon, Gwendolyn Riley, and Penny Vaden reigned from 1953 to 1955.

Judith Jamison, Joyce Graves (see Plate 26), and Donna Lowe Warren emerged between 1955 and 1958. China White (formerly known as Melva Murray White), and Sally Anne Richardson emerged from 1958 to 1962. In the early 1960s to the mid-1960s, Renee Wadley, Robby Green, Tina Johnson, and Myrna Munchus, were lead dancers and Debra Bland, Tawny Turner, and Carol Treherne were promising dancers from the mid-1960s to 1971 (M.D. Cuyjet, personal communication, November, 1984, to April, 1986).

According to Judith Jamison, a friendly competitive spirit existed among Judimar female lead dancers, but the desire to be recognized as the best never became a destructive force that endangered friendships (personal communication, May 16, 1985). The advanced female dancers were important role models for the younger students. Lowe states: "Delores was my idol. Many of the young dancers wanted to be like her" (personal communication, September 28, 1985).

Accompanists

All the dance classes at Judimar were accompanied by live music from 1948 to 1959. Cuyjet secured a pianist for ballet, tap, and jazz classes. (In the late 1940s and early 1950s, there were no phonograph records produced specifically to accompany dance classes.) John Hines was in charge of the percussionists for the Primitive and interpretive classes and recitals (M.D. Cuyjet, personal communication, November 29, 1984). Bernice Gardner was Judimar's first pianist. She was recommended to Cuyjet by someone who knew the school was in need of an accompanist and she began playing in 1948. Gardner doubled as an assistant teacher and pianist when playing for Cuyjet's tap classes. Cuyjet fondly remembers Gardner:

> She started with me when I first opened at 1310 Walnut. I was the only teacher then. Bernice loved those dancing classes so much. I ran a "change your hat" business during those days. While teaching class, if the telephone rang, I'd have to answer it. So Bernice brought a pair of tap shoes and wore them for tap class. The parents laughed at her. I

> never responded when they mentioned it to me. The first time I had to leave the class to answer the telephone [I was gone five or ten minutes], Bernice left the piano and continued class. They [the children] never got a break. In most classes if the teacher has to leave the room, they know they are going to have a few minutes to roam around. Not with Bernice—she even had the proper intonations when verbalizing tap rhythms. (personal communication, September 11, 1985)

Gardner played for numerous churches in Black Philadelphia. She left the school in 1951 when her schedule became too demanding. Alice Davis, an aspiring concert pianist, replaced Gardner. She played for recitals as well as classes. Cuyjet describes Davis as a temperamental artist who refused to play if the children talked during class. She remained at the school until 1959.

Judimar's main percussionists were Garvin Masseaux and Bobby (Robert) Crowder (see Plate 19). Both men studied with Saka Ackquye and were considered master drummers (J. Hines, personal communication, July 24, 1985). According to music historian, the late Harrison Ridley, Jr., they were members of an elite group of percussionists who established Black Philadelphia as a "Mecca" of African drumming in the 1950s, (personal communication, October 17, 1985) Additional drummers were Sam Morgan, John Arnez, Manning H. Mosley, Jr., and Fredrick Campbell. Campbell was a sculptor and painter who made all the school's percussion instruments and gave instruction in drum construction for the boys (M.D. Cuyjet, personal communication, February 13, 1986).

Administration

Cuyjet rarely handled the business aspects of the school between 1948 and 1958. Before classes began each day, she divided her time between studying student progress folders, going over pedagogy notes, and revising lesson plans for student teachers. Cuyjet's primary function outside of the classroom was to monitor student development and choreograph for recitals and community performances.

Cuyjet studied each progress folder carefully making notes when necessary. The folders included an evaluation form, a small photograph of the child, and a section for attendance. She was particularly strict with punctuality. Children were sent to the office for tardiness. "We did this because at this time children came to our school on public transportation. We reprimanded them for their protection" (M.D. Cuyjet, personal communication, April 3, 1986).

Stephen Cuyjet was Judimar's senior administrator until his illness in the late 1950s. He relieved his wife of many of the details of operating the school so she could be free to teach and choreograph (E. Ball, personal communication, September 4, 1985). Stephen Cuyjet, Jr. describes his father's role at Judimar:

> He was the business manager. Mother was the artist. He ran the books, settled disputes between students, was in charge of transportation when we performed in the community, collected tuition, and called parents who were delinquent with their payments. In addition to his responsibilities at the school he worked full time at the post office and was a regular substitute industrial arts teacher for the Philadelphia Public Schools. One of the reasons the school was so successful was that mother did not have to avert her attention. (personal communication, March 1, 1986)

Frances Jimenez was the school's head administrative officer (registrar and secretary) from 1950 to 1957. Cuyjet, assisted by her mother, Frances Durham, handled administrative responsibilities from 1958 to 1971.

Strategies for Survival

Judimar School remained in existence for 23 years. During that time, the major issues of survival revolved around securing a permanent studio space and achieving economic stability.

Early in this chapter, Cuyjet describes herself as a pioneer because she established her first school in a predominately white business district of Center City Philadelphia. Most of her landlords assumed that she was white. When they discovered that she served Black children, Cuyjet stressed the fact that Judimar was interracial, in hopes of convincing them to grant her substantial leasing terms. Cuyjet was not easily discouraged when asked to vacate her studios. She simply found another one in the same vicinity. Her lawyer was usually available to intervene and make suggestions in case of difficulty. A transient "track record" could create enrollment problems for most schools, yet, according to Judith Jamison, students followed Cuyjet each time the school relocated during the first decade of its existence (Lecture demonstration, February 10, 1985).

Achieving economic stability was a constant problem because funding for private dance schools has never existed. Cuyjet depended on tuition to operate the school. There was never enough to pay all the expenses when due. Stephen Cuyjet usually supplemented the tuition. "We depended on tuition and my husband's paycheck. There would be times I would run to Steve and ask for his paycheck. He would step back and say: "Not again!" (M.D. Cuyjet, personal communication, February 13, 1986).

There were never any massive fundraising campaigns. Cuyjet avoided them. She knew the parents would not consent. "Our clientele would have objected to large fundraising ventures on this pretext: 'We pay tuition'" (M.D. Cuyjet, personal communication, February, 1986). Judimar barely survived on tuition (S. Cuyjet, Jr., personal communication, March 1, 1986). In the 1950s, the parents established a "Mothers Club" for the purpose of raising funds for the recital and for scholarships. There was 80% participation. The club was discontinued in the 1960s (J. Colvin, personal communication, September 7, 1985).

Recital ticket sales provided funds to pay for space rental and production personnel. Tickets were usually three dollars. In 1955, Judimar held a ticket contest. The first prizewinner received the honor of having their picture on the cover of the recital bulletin. The winner, Ronald Platts, later pursued a career as a dancer and teacher (Judimar School, Recital Bulletin, June 17, 1955).

In the 1950s, a few local businesses underwrote tickets to some of the performances. The following program note appeared on the back of the Judimar recital bulletin on June 18, 1954:

> WE ARE INDEED GRATEFUL TO THE FOLLOWING MEN FOR UNDERWRITING TICKETS TO THIS PERFORMANCE FOR CHILDREN OF THE BUREAU FOR COLORED CHILDREN, THE CATHOLIC CHILDREN'S BUREAU, AND THE WOMEN'S CHRISTIAN ALLIANCE CENTER.
>
> Franklin P. Ryan, Electrical Contractor, J.H. Shepher, Plumbing and Heating Contractor, James Green, Registered Cement Worker, Harold Treegoob, Treegoob Furniture and Appliances.

Performance Outlets

Performance was a significant aspect of the Judimar experience. Cuyjet placed a premium on performance, and she took advantage of most opportunities which became available. Stephen Cuyjet, Jr. states:

> My mother is a firm believer that dance is a performing art. You can't rehearse it to death. You can't be a dancer if you only dance in front of a mirror. So if you were one of her students, you performed, not only in the recitals, but in elementary schools, high schools, for social clubs, civic organizations, and cabarets. (personal communication, March 1, 1986)

If an honorarium were involved, it paid for transportation, or was added to the school's general fund. "It cost us money to perform, but it was a form of advertising for us" (M.D Cuyjet, personal communication, November 29, 1984). Cuyjet viewed community performances as a civic duty. The following recital program note makes reference to performances during the late 1940s and the early 1950s.

> The Judimar School of Dance recognized its responsibility to the public and yearly groups of students perform at civic and charitable affairs, as well as the public school system. To be remembered are the performances given at the Christian Street Branch YMCA, the Kensington Branch YWCA, Fiesta, sponsored by the Germantown Civic League, the Community Center of West Chester, Pa., the Cultural Olympics of the University of Pennsylvania, numerous appearances at U.S. Army Recreation and Rehabilitation centers. Notable was the performance of the *Sleeping Beauty* ballet at the Douglass-Singerly Public School, 22nd and Norris Streets—four performances in one day'! (Judimar School, Recital Bulletin, June n.d., 1950)

In the early 1950s, Judimar students began to perform beyond the boundaries of Black Philadelphia. They auditioned for Eugene Ormandy for a chance to participate in the youth concert series for the Philadelphia Orchestra. The group was not chosen to perform, yet a program note describes the audition as a "red letter" day in Judimar history:

> This audition was of great importance for the Philadelphia artistic world as never before had a Negro group auditioned for such a berth. Mr. Ormandy commended the group for its competence and poise. (Judimar School, Recital Bulletin, June n.d., 1950)

Additional performance outlets included church teas, fashion shows, Delta Sigma Theta Sorority revues (The Jabberwock), and out-of-state performances at Delaware State College, Cheyney State College, and Maryland State College.

On occasion, an ensemble would perform for musical organizations. In 1952, the group performed in the Dra Mu Opera's production of *Carmen* and in 1954, *Samson and Delilah*. In the Winter of 1954, they performed with the National Negro Opera Company and the Pittsburgh Symphony in *Aida* at the Syria Mosque in Pittsburgh, Pennsylvania. Mention of their performance appeared in a *Pittsburg Courier* review:

> Among the best features of the opera was a spirited, virile, ballet with Joe Nash, Delores Browne, and John Jones as leads. (J. Nash, personal communication, August 16, 1985)

Cuyjet formed a performing unit for the advanced dancers in 1953. In its initial stages, Joe Nash and Ernest Parham were in charge of choreography. The group was known as The Judimar Theatre Dance Company. Members included Vera Bass, Samuel Carruthers, Yvonne Green, Franca Jimenez, Marie Jimenez, Doris Keith, Delores Browne, Ione Nash, Ronald Platts, George Williams, and Shirley Spicer (Judimar School, Recital Bulletin, June 18, 1954).

In the early 1950s, some of Judimar's advanced dancers along with dancers from the Sydney and Eleanois schools of dance appeared on the Dave Garroway *Today* show on location at the Philadelphia Museum of Art. An article describing the event appeared in the Philadelphia edition of *The Afro-American* (M.D. Cuyjet, Private Collection). Joe Nash, choreographer for the event, briefly describes the performances:

> A jazz band [the Billy Krechner Ensemble] was playing inside of the museum while the dancers danced around the fountain. The camera created a kaleidoscopic effect. The dancers and the band appeared alternately inside of a painting. (personal communication, August 16, 1985)

In the 1960s, Judimar students performed for numerous elementary and secondary schools in Philadelphia and the tri-state area. In addition, selected advanced students appeared on *Wiffil Schoolhouse* and *Blackboard*, WFIL educational T.V. programs (see Plate 27).

In 1963, two of Judimar's advanced female dancers performed with the Capital Ballet Company (The Capital Ballet Guild, Inc.) in Washington, D.C. The following letter from Doris Jones, and Claire Haywood, directors of the company, is a thank you correspondence to Cuyjet:

> This is just a note to say that Miss Jones and I deeply appreciate your cooperation in allowing us to work with your students. We have written to Doris Hering of *Dance Magazine*, Mrs. Virginia Wershberger, Mr. Alan Banks, Mr. Chaffee, Mrs. Virginia Williams [Boston], and The School of American Ballet—asking their cooperation, also. Many teachers realize that there are not too many opportunities for the young

> Negro classic ballet dancer. This foundation in Washington seems very anxious to help them, not only as company members, but also with many other educational opportunities in the related arts and sciences.
>
> I hope that the two boys who are coming are as talented as your two girls.
>
> Once more, thank you. We are still anxious to visit your school. It would have been sooner, but we just finished the choreography for Howard University's *Fly Blackbird.* (M.D. Cuyjet, Private Collection)

The most important performance outlets were the Philadelphia Cotillion Society's annual Christmas Cotillions and the school's annual spring recital.

The professionalism with which Cuyjet approached her teaching and the management of the school pervaded the manner in which she staged the Judimar recitals. She was assisted by a dedicated parent, family, and friend production team. The recitals were lavish productions. Attention was given to lighting, staging, with emphasis on costumes and music. Addece Riley and Laura Vaden, whose children were enrolled at the school, constructed the costumes with the assistance of a team of mothers. Judy Cuyjet occasionally drew preliminary costume sketches.

In the 1950s, a small orchestra, conducted by Vito La Monica, provided the musical accompaniment. Stephen Cuyjet, Jr. remarks:

> She used an orchestra for her ballets as long as she could. We began with about 13 pieces. As the cost went up the number of musicians decreased. She was a purest. She wanted strings for the ballets. She kept that tradition as long as it was financially feasible. (personal communication, March 1, 1986)

Judimar discontinued using an orchestra in the 1960s. Cuyjet occasionally secured Bernie Berle (a local musician) and his band, but usually hired a sound technician to prepare an audio tape.

Cuyjet was adamant about compiling recital bulletins which complemented the production. They were well planned, thorough, with copious program notes.

They included a story synopsis of each ballet and an explanation of ballet terms for the roles performed by dancers (Judimar School, Recital Bulletin, June 1950). The recitals were viewed as major events in Black Philadelphia. In the late 1940s and the early 1950s, they were held at the Broad Street Branch Young Men's and Women's Hebrew Association in the Fleisher Auditorium. In 1952, Judimar secured the Met Theatre on Broad and Poplar Streets and from 1953 to 1970 they were staged at Town Hall. In 1971 the final recital was held at the YM-YWHA (J. Colvin, personal communication, September 7, 1985).

The goal of each recital was to produce an entertaining show and to showcase the children's dance development. The "Cuyjet recital formula" involved writing an original scenario which revolved around a theme or creating one based on a well-known ballet or Broadway musical. Stephen Cuyjet, Jr. elaborates:

> One year we did a ballet based on the concept of the corner drug store. The characters we played were the articles found in a drug store. Some of the girls represented various perfumes or cosmetics. I was the soda jerk, and a friend of mine was Charles of the Ritz. He did a tap number. When she did musicals she would use only the published music so she would not have to pay for the rights of the play. We did *West Side Story* but renamed it *On the Block*. She rewrote the story line a bit. In the sixties we combined the basic ideas from *Oklahoma* and *Seven Brides for Seven Brothers* and created a ballet called *Barn Raising*. (personal communication, March 1, 1986)

Additional recital pieces included Cinderella, Swan Lake, Peter Pan, The Red Shoes, The Black Doll, Carmen with the Esten Collins Singers, Giselle, Carnivale, and L'eau Tropique.

Cuyjet was responsible for the majority of the choreography for the main production numbers. Her teachers and guest choreographers assisted with jazz, tap, modern, Afro-Caribbean, and ballet numbers. In the 1960s, guest choreographers included George Chaffee, Jay Dash, Carl Sandemar, Joan Myers Brown, and former students Delores Browne Abelson, Judy Cuyjet Colvin, and Elmer Ball.

The first segment of the program usually featured the advanced dancers. The accomplished female students were given a "debut." They would perform a solo or pas de deux with a leading male student. Cuyjet chose a Judimar prima ballerina every few years. Among those chosen were Judith Jamison, Joyce Graves, Donna Lowe Warren, Judith Cuyjet, China White, and Tawny Turner. The second portion featured one or two dance suites and each child in the school was included.

The recital embraced a total theater concept. Students played characters and were occasionally required to sing. "We knew how to act and dance before we got to New York" (E. Ball, personal communication, September 4, 1985). Judimar recitals were bold and costly ventures. During the 1950s and 1960s virtually no other dance schools in Black Philadelphia, with the exception of Sydney School of Dance, were producing full-scale recital productions.

Former Students; Ramifications of the Legacy

This section will focus on Delores Browne Abelson, Donna Lowe Warren, Judith Jamison, and Elmer Ball, former students who pursued professional dance careers and continued to perpetuate the dance preparation they received at the Judimar School of Dance.

Delores Browne Abelson

Browne's initial interest in dance was spurred at age nine by Hollywood dance movies of the mid-1940s. She briefly discusses the circumstances under which she sought dance training:

> My family could not afford to give me dance lessons. That was totally out of our reach. My aunt said that if I found a school that would take me that she would pay for my lessons. This was in the late 1940s. I went to every school that was established in center city. I lived at 22nd and Ordain [South Philadelphia], so at that time I could walk to

> everywhere in the general Center City area. They put me on a waiting list. I was too young to understand what that meant. I was never called. (personal communication, August 23, 1985)

Browne decided to attend Barratt Junior High School in part because it offered dance. She joined the ballet club. She states: "When I got that opportunity, that was one in a million" (personal communication, August 23, 1985).

Browne received a scholarship to Judimar in 1948. Her recollection of the occasion is similar to Cuyjet's. She comments:

> Cuyjet had just broken up with King. She was starting out on her own and wanted some advanced students when she started. She visited Barratt Junior High School. She contacted Lingenfelder, the director of the dance club. She requested two of the top students in the club. They happened to be Alice Mays and Juanita Jones. The teacher asked Cuyjet if she would take one more, a student who was a hard worker, that was me. I had been studying just about six months. I was a year younger than the other two girls. She took all three of us on full scholarship. (personal communication, August 23, 1985)

Browne's Judimar experience began at age 14. She progressed at an astounding rate. In six months time she was chosen for the lead role in *Sleeping Beauty.* In retrospect, Browne is amazed at Cuyjet's ability to work miracles with young people who began their ballet training at what was considered a late age.

During the initial stages of her training, she attended Judimar twice a week. By the time she was 17, she was there every day. She studied ballet (pointe and partnering) with Cuyjet, and Dunham with John Hines. She studied tap but admits that her aptitude was low (personal communication, August 23, 1985). She studied ballet with the guest teachers who frequented the school and was always included on the New York trips to Ballet Arts and the Dunham School (White-Dixon, 1995, p. 305).

Browne's parents were supportive of her dance endeavors. They frequently allowed her to get a head start on the New York trips by arriving early to begin classes. "My father paid extra for me to go early. I stayed at the "Y". John Hines and George Mills were in New York at that time, so I had people to look out for me" (D.B. Abelson, August 23, 1985).

Browne describes her teacher/pupil relationship with Cuyjet in the following way: "I think she saw something special in me and helped me develop it" (personal communication, August 23, 1985). Cuyjet's desire to produce Black ballerinas during an era when there were few came to fruition through Browne. She was Cuyjet's first student to dance professionally.

According to Browne, the Judimar School was ahead of its time. She comments:

> Judimar was wonderful. It was run very professionally. It was the cream of the crop, not just for me. It attracted a lot of people. One of the great things is that we were able to be partnered by men for our performances. That was exciting for me. We had quite a few boys and men. Most schools during that time rarely had male students. They dressed girls as boys for their recitals. In addition, recitals were quite ambitious. She was an incredibly gutsy lady with what she did with the productions. We had professionally made costumes and an orchestra. When we did *Swan Lake*, she imported the original musical score from Europe by courier. George Chaffee came and helped Cuyjet set the ballet. (personal communication, August 23, 1985)

One of the most attractive features of the school was the opportunity to perform. Browne danced for recitals, cotillions, and numerous community performances. She was chosen to perform with the Dra Mu Opera Company for their production of *Carmen* (see Plate 28) and with the National Negro Opera Company in *Aida*. Her most memorable performing experience was the 1955 Christmas Cotillion production of the *Blue Venus*. Browne states: "I was the Pearl. It was thrilling, the whole production was exhilarating" (personal communication, August 23, 1985).

Browne left Judimar in 1953 to go to New York to pursue professional dance preparation. She was 17 years of age and had just graduated from West Philadelphia High School. The Judimar Mothers Club offered her financial assistance for her studies. Browne comments on the support she received from Judimar:

> The Mothers Club was strong then. Judy's (Judith Jamison) mother was one of the leaders in that club. They gave me the money to go to the School of American Ballet. They said if I got through the audition that they would pay my tuition for a year. They did just that. I got into the advanced class and they paid the tuition for the first year in New York. That was the kind of support I started out with. (personal communication, August 23, 1985)

Browne returned to Philadelphia after the first year because of family problems. She decided to return to New York a few years later (around 1956) and enrolled at the Ballet Theatre School. During that period she joined the New York Negro Ballet Company (Ballet Americana) (see Plate 29). She performed with the company for two years and during that time they toured Great Britain. She then began to perform with Louis Johnson, Alvin Ailey, and Geoffrey Holder. "At that time they did not have companies like we have today. There were no years of employment. We did concerts and tours. You were employed and then [you were] out of work" (personal communication, August 23, 1985). During this time she continued her dance studies. She remembers studying with Karel Shook at night after rehearsals. In between her performances Browne taught ballet. She states:

> I had always taught, and liked it. It was a way to earn money and stay in the business. I taught ballet for Syvilla Fort. I was capable of teaching Dunham, but I had moved away from it. I decided to stay with ballet. (personal communication, August 23, 1985)

Browne places a premium on the dance preparation she received at Judimar. She comments:

> I still fall back on my Judimar training. It was the strongest foundation for me. When I first went to the School of American Ballet, I was one of the few people trained outside of New York that had a good

> background in ballet terminology. I studied with several teachers after Judimar, but I don't remember being as impressed as I was with what I received at Judimar. I remember strengthening my training, I remember being coached, but not necessarily learning something new. I kept falling back on the training I received at Judimar. (personal communication, August 23, 1985)

Browne joined the staff of the Alvin Ailey American Dance Center in the early 1970s and assumed the post as scholarship director and taught advanced ballet until the late 1970s. In the mid-1970s, she began teaching for Philadanco.

Browne states that Cuyjet has had a profound influence on her own teaching style and approach. She briefly discusses that influence:

> I am also very specific about being on time for classes, training the whole person, stressing the importance of knowing your craft. I'm pretty tough about those things. I don't think that when you are taking class that you should take a frivolous attitude about it. It's too important even if it is for your own amusement. I've taught adult ballet. When I teach these classes I teach them as if I feel they are going to do something with it. (personal communication, August 23, 1985)

From the 1980s to the 1990s, Browne devoted her full-time energies to operating a successful native American art gallery in New York City. She continues to travel to Philadelphia once a week to teach company ballet class for Philadanco.

Donna Lowe Warren

Donna Lowe Warren is a native of Brooklyn, New York but was raised in Philadelphia by her aunt. Lowe's aunt enrolled her in Judimar for formal dance preparation at age five. She began by attending class once a week on Saturdays and as she advanced in level, she was in attendance several days a week. She studied ballet with Delores Browne Abelson, selected guest teachers, and tap with Ann Bernadino Hughes and John Hines. Her advanced ballet classes were taken with Cuyjet (see Plate 30). Warren states that although Cuyjet's stern teaching manner was sometimes intimidating, she enjoyed her classes regardless. She states: "She scared us a bit, but we loved her classes. She made us want to dance" (personal communication, September 28, 1985).

She speaks of her Judimar experience as the highlight of her childhood and teenage years: "I remember being so very happy there. It was one big family and we all knew we were there for one purpose—to dance" (D.L. Warren, personal communication, September 28, 1985). Warren emerged as a leading dancer in the mid-1950s and was given her debut at age 15 (see Plate 31). She comments:

> Cuyjet staged *Giselle* for me. That was my most memorable experience. It was quite an honor to have my first classic role in a ballet of note. I received roses afterwards. (personal communication, September 28, 1985)

Warren participated in all of the Judimar performance events and enrichment activities except for the trips to New York. In the mid-1950s, she studied there with George Chaffee during her annual summer vacation with her parents.

Warren left Judimar in the late 1950s. Cuyjet advised her to study with Thomas Cannon, who was at that time ballet master for the Philadelphia Grand Opera Company. Cannon chose Lowe as a member of the opera's ballet unit in 1958. During an era when Philadelphia's professional ballet arena remained closed to African Americans, Warren's fair complexion enabled Cannon to pass her off as white. She performed in the corps, then as a soloist. Warren reflects on her experiences with the company:

> I toured many cities with the opera company. New York, Boston, Miami, and Tulsa were a few. It was an exciting time for me. We worked with the great singers of the day like Richard Tucker and Roberta Peters. This was a new aspect of theater for me. Still because I had been exposed to Judimar's elaborate productions at an early age I was not flabbergasted when I arrived in the professional world. (personal communication, September 28, 1985)

In the early 1960s, Warren decided to continue her education. She auditioned for Julliard's ballet program, was accepted, and received a partial scholarship for her first year. Although her major emphasis was ballet, she was required to study modern and recalls studying with celebrated dancers Martha Graham and José Limon. In addition, there were classes in composition, Labanotation, and kinesiology. She discontinued her studies after the first year because her parents were unable to afford full tuition, and the commute from Brooklyn was taking its toll (D.L. Warren, personal communication, September 28, 1985).

Warren returned to Philadelphia and transferred to St. Joseph's University and majored in social studies. She resumed her position with the Philadelphia Grand Opera Company and moved up the ranks to prima ballerina status. She remained with the company until 1971.

In 1982, Warren opened the Philadelphia School of Dance in Lehigh Acres, Florida. She comments:

> I feel like a pioneer bringing dance to this area. Most have not been exposed to ballet. The community has responded positively. The "Y" is no longer in existence so the parents were glad to have a place for their children to go. (personal communication, September 28, 1985)

The school is expanding and now offers instruction in ballet (with pointe), tap, jazz, baton, and gymnastics. She envisions establishing a regional ballet company. Warren invited Cuyjet to Florida as a guest speaker for the opening of the school. She states: "I wanted her here to share this special occasion with me. She is extremely instrumental in my development" (personal communication, September 28, 1985).

Judith Jamison

Judith Jamison entered Judimar in 1950 at the age of six. Her mother strongly believed that dance was an essential artistic experience for children. Jamison states that her parents played an important role in her artistic development. Her father was an accomplished musician and her mother was an avid theater enthusiast and collector of graphic art (Maynard, 1982, p. 16).

According to Cuyjet, Jamison displayed natural dance ability from the start of her studies. She was viewed as a prodigy. When Jamison entered Judimar, Cuyjet recalls having a heated argument with John Hines because he wanted to place her in the second grade (level) (Faggins, February 8, 1985, p. 8).

Jamison traveled to Judimar several times a week from her home in the Germantown section of Philadelphia. She studied ballet, tap, Primitive, jazz, and acrobatics (see Plate 32). Although she loathed acrobatics, she applauded the school's policy of requiring students to take a variety of movement techniques. "Cuyjet made well-rounded dancers" (J. Jamison, personal communication, May 16, 1985). Her teachers included Cuyjet, Delores Browne Abelson, John Jones, Elmer Ball (ballet), John Hines (Dunham), Ann Bernadino Hughes (tap) and Ernest Parham (modern and jazz).

Jamison was impressed with the manner in which Judimar was managed. She states:

> The school was very professional—the recitals and the way in which classes were conducted. She prepared me for a professional life even before I knew I was going to dance. (personal communication, May 16, 1985)

According to Jamison, Judimar possessed a unique environment. She comments:

> We learned how to dance, and to teach. In addition Cuyjet created a world within the school, social as well as educational. She'd give these little parties—quite formal and polite, you know—and she'd match the right gentleman with the right lady. (Goldner, February 9, 1985, p. 1-D)

Jamison participated in recitals, community performances, and Christmas Cotillions. Just before she graduated from high school she received the Cotillion

Society's dance award. Cuyjet comments on her performance savvy in a 1974 *Philadelphia Inquirer* article:

> She stuck to the choreography, but she added her artistry to it, which astounded me because the role always came off looking like something different than I planned...and usually better. (Sims, n.m., n.d., 1974)

Jamison's formal debut was in 1959 at age 15. She danced the role of Myrtha in *Giselle* (see Plate 31).

After graduating from Germantown High School, she decided to pursue a college degree. Cuyjet assisted her in securing admission and a partial scholarship at Fisk University in Nashville, Tennessee and she remained at the school for a year. Her goal of becoming a psychologist became less important than her desire to dance. She returned to Philadelphia in the early 1960s to continue her dance training and entered the Philadelphia Dance Academy (presently University of the Arts). In 1964, Agnes de Mille discovered her in a master class at the Academy and invited her to come to New York to perform in the *Four Marys*. That initial exposure paved the way for her entrance to the professional dance world. She comments:

> I wanted to be a fine dancer. I had been performing since I was six and I wanted to perform more. New York was a mecca. All I thought about was getting better at what I was doing and performing more. So whoever heard of getting your first job in New York with ABT (American Ballet Theatre)—understudying Carmen de Lavallade! I've been blessed. But the perseverance was instilled in me by my parents and Marion Cuyjet. (Goldner, February 9, 1985, p. 3-D)

In 1965, Jamison joined the Alvin Ailey American Dance Theater and remained with the company for 15 years. She emerged as its leading female dancer and established herself as an international dance star. She left the company in 1980 to assume the starring role in the Broadway musical *Sophisticated Ladies*.

Jamison began developing her skills as a choreographer and teacher and in 1984 the Ailey company premiered her first dance work, *Divining*. During the

1980s, she devoted a great deal of time teaching master workshops nationwide and teaching advanced students at the Alvin Ailey American Dance Center. In April 1985, she taught a five-day technique/performance workshop, for the Temple University Department of Dance. During the workshop her teaching disposition was firm and direct. She admits that her manner has been influenced by Cuyjet. She comments: "Cuyjet was very strict. I believe that is why she turned out so many serious students. It [Cuyjet's disciplinary teaching style] carried over to my teaching" (personal communication, May 16, 1985).

Jamison continues to perpetuate the Judimar emphasis on nurturing expressive dancers. The following excerpt elaborates:

> In my coaching sessions at the Ailey School I'm trying to make advanced students blossom beyond only technique. Technical dancers are boring. I try to get them closer to their uniqueness. The most gratifying moments when I was with Ailey were to see a dancer figure out that there's only one of him. When that happens, the floodgates open. You get depth. (Goldner, February 9, 1985, p. 3-D).

Elmer Ball

Elmer M. Ball Jr. (AKA "Skeets") graduated from West Philadelphia High School in 1953 at age 17. His initial dance preparation occurred during his freshman year in college at Howard University in Washington, D.C. The directors of the renowned Jones-Haywood Ballet School, Doris Jones and Claire Haywood, recruited several students from Howard's drama department for a production of *Finian's Rainbow*. Ball was one of those chosen. His major interest was dramatic arts, yet the directors of the school vowed to transform him into a dancer. During rehearsals for the production, Ball began his formal dance training at the Jones-Haywood School of Dance.

Ball decided to leave school in order to pursue his interest in dance. Two friends (Charles Medley and Charles Moore) from Philadelphia, suggested that he enter Judimar. Cuyjet accepted him on scholarship. According to Cuyjet, Ball developed at an astounding rate considering he began ballet training at what was considered a late age (personal communication, November 25, 1985). He studied at Judimar from 1953 to 1959. During the same time period, he studied (on weekends and summers) with Philadelphia and New York dance educators including, Tom Cannon, Antony Tudor, Valentina Pereyaslavec, Pearl Primus, Syvilla Fort, Jack Cole, and Matt Mattox (E. Ball, personal communication, September 4, 1985).

When Ball enrolled at Judimar in 1953, there were already several male students. He states: "The competition between the men was fierce. Many of them were fine dancers. One in particular was McCoy Tyner [a nationally known jazz pianist who performed with John Coltrane] (see Plate 19). He left the school and later pursued a career in music" (personal communication, September 4, 1985).

Ball was completely immersed in his dance studies and attended school five to six hours a day several times a week. He states:

> I don't think any of us thought about what we would become or what we would make out of it [dance]. Many of the male students' parents objected to their sons' involvement in dance and could not understand the fascination with it. They were mystified by our passion for something that did not assure immediate financial reward. (personal communication, September 4, 1985)

Ball states that he viewed Judimar as a sacred institution. He comments:

> We were all very dedicated to Judimar, yet I saw Judimar in another light. I spent many hours at the school cleaning up after everyone had left. It seemed like a church to me. That is how intense my feelings were. (personal communication, September 4, 1985)

Ball emerged as one of Judimar's leading male dancers in the late 1950s (see Plate 33). His forte was ballet. It takes several years of training to attain a professional level of ballet proficiency. Ball developed at a rapid pace and became an advanced-level ballet student despite his limited years of study and was considered a premier dancer within Judimar's non-professional school setting. According to him, Cuyjet groomed him to be her daughter's main dance partner. "Judy Cuyjet was the school's prima ballerina (see Plate 34). Donna Lowe and Judith Jamison were good, but Judy was special because of her acting ability" (E. Ball, personal communication, September 4, 1985).

The teacher-pupil relationship Ball and Cuyjet shared was a special one. Ball states:

> Cuyjet was like a mother to me. I accompanied her to Delaware for her classes at Delaware State College. She wanted me to go back to college, but I wanted to dance. She told me that I had plenty of time to dance, but get that piece of paper [a degree]. (personal communication, September 4, 1985)

Ball decided to go to New York to pursue a professional dance career in the fall of 1959. He was there one week before he found a job. He auditioned and was accepted into the Dunham Company. "I knew I was ready. Judimar prepared me well" (personal communication, September 4, 1985). He performed with the company from 1959 to 1960 (see Plate 35). During that period, they toured Denmark, Germany, Holland, and France. He gradually learned the Dunham Technique from Linwood Morris, the ballet master and leading dancer.

Ball left the Dunham Company in 1960, and returned to Philadelphia. Cuyjet asked him to teach jazz for her at the Jay Dash studio. The experience was extremely rewarding, but Ball longed for the energy of New York. He states: "Cuyjet again approached me about going to college at Maryland State College where Judy was, but I wanted to get back to New York where the action was" (personal communication, September 4, 1985).

In the early 1960s, Ball performed with the Louis Johnson Dance Company, the Talley Beatty Dance Company, The Alvin Ailey Dance Company (1962 Africa Tour), and the Trockadero Gloxinia Ballet. During his career he took the stage name of Matthew Cameron. From the mid-1960s to the late-1970s, he performed in Off Broadway musicals under the direction of Vinette Carroll, Hazel Bryant, and Joseph Papp (see Plate 36).

Ball left New York in 1976 and embarked on a career as a teacher and choreographer in Philadelphia. He has taught for Joan Myers Brown, the Philadelphia College of Performing Arts (presently University of the Arts), Joan Kerr, and the Tri-State Ballet. He also served as ballet master of Freedom Theater's dance department. Ball, who passed in 1988, comments on Cuyjet's influence on his teaching endeavors and his role in perpetuating her legacy: "I pattern my classes after Cuyjet's. She is a brilliant teacher. I think it is our [former students'] job to carry on her legacy" (personal communication, September 4, 1985).

Additional former Judimar students who have continued their involvement in dance through performance and/or education included Judith Cuyjet, Gail Nelson, China White, John Jones, Cheryl Jenkins, Myrna (Amai) Munchus-Bullock, Helen Riley, Janice Harrison, Tamara Guillebeaux, Patricia Scott-Hobbs, Tawny Turner, Charles Moore, and Ronald Platts (see Appendix B).

Marion Cuyjet and the Judimar School of Dance touched the lives of a great number of youth in Black Philadelphia from 1948 to 1971. Informal interviews with several former students reveal that they credit Judimar with playing a vital role in their personal growth and development. Many of them state that their Judimar experience helped them cultivate the discipline and the positive self-image needed to survive in the "real world" and in their chosen profession.

Judimar's organizational structure was similar to some of the professional schools in which Cuyjet had studied and reflected her early exposure through Essie Marie Dorsey. She operated the school with the devout support of her family and friends and her staff was composed of accomplished dance educators, musicians, and professional dancer-educators from the New York dance arena. Judimar provided a positive and creative environment in which Black dancers and dance educators, and musicians could realize their full potential.

Judimar was established during a period in which Black Philadelphians were adamant about improving their quality of life. The climate of the times had a great impact on the ideals which Cuyjet promoted at her school. She, too, was concerned with social, cultural, educational, political, and economic advancement. In response to this issue Cuyjet addressed the personal, social, cultural, and educational development of her students, and nurtured them to be the "best" in all of their endeavors.

Delores Browne Abelson, Donna Lowe Warren, Judith Jamison, and Elmer Ball are dancer-educators who continued to perpetuate the dance preparation which they received at the Judimar School. According to these dancers and several other former students interviewed, they are grateful for their Judimar preparation because it shaped them as artists, educators, and most importantly, achievers.

The Judimar School was formed, expanded, relocated, struggled, and survived for two decades through the determination and perseverance of Marion Cuyjet. It represented a pinnacle of achievement for Cuyjet and an important contribution toward the cultural and educational life of Black Philadelphia.

CHAPTER 5

Vision and Legacy

Cuyjet's vision was rooted in her desire to provide concert dance preparation for youth in Black Philadelphia. As a result of her efforts, she emerged as a renowned teacher and a vital force in shaping dance education in Black Philadelphia. Her adept teaching ability enabled her to produce proficient dancers and dance educators, and her school became a symbol of high achievement standards and artistic integrity.

Black Philadelphia supported Cuyjet's endeavors from the outset of her professional teaching career. During this post-war era, Americans were more familiar with show dancing (Broadway, Vaudeville, night clubs) than with concert dance forms and techniques. In Black Philadelphia, the groundwork for the acceptance of concert dance and formal dance studies had been established in the late 1920s by Cuyjet's mentor, Essie Marie Dorsey.

Cuyjet maintained an active career as a distinguished teacher and leading proponent of dance education in Black Philadelphia for 23 years. How and why was she able to achieve such a distinction?

Cuyjet's initial interest in dance was purely recreational. Her experiences with the Alma Polk Kiddie Revue, her junior high school folk dance club, and exposure to Dorsey's early dance recitals affected her motivation. Her decision to seek entrance into the Dorsey school was prompted by peer influence and a desire to continue her favorite leisure activity. Cuyjet did not possess enough money for transportation, an invitation, or permission from her parents to attend the Dorsey school opening. Her predicament did not discourage her, and she went anyway. This incident represents Cuyjet's first significant initiative toward pursuing her interest in dance. Her determination was one of the elements which helped her then and would be a mainstay as she continued her career in dance.

Cuyjet's experiences at the Dorsey school broadened her perception of dance. She discovered a codified system of dance movement that required a great deal of physical and mental discipline. She accepted the challenge with vigor. Her special friendship with Sydney King served to strengthen her bond with dance and the two young girls developed an ideal reciprocal support system.

Cuyjet's desire and initiative exceeded her technical ability, but she was an excellent student and novice teacher. Her junior high school physical education teacher, Virginia Lingenfelder, described Cuyjet's dance aptitude by stating that she "moved in six different directions while dancing." Dorsey, however, had a positive vision of Cuyjet's capabilities, and provided her with a great deal of motivation and support. It was as if she transferred the hopes and dreams she once held for herself to Cuyjet. Dorsey's aspirations to dance professionally were dwarfed because of the exclusion of Blacks in the concert dance arena. She seized the opportunity to provide Cuyjet a method of entering the ballet world regardless of its discriminatory policies. She passed the fair-skinned Cuyjet off as white and enrolled her in a well-known Philadelphia ballet school in the late 1930s. Although Cuyjet was dismissed from the school when they discovered her true racial identity, Dorsey, undaunted by the incident, continued to invest in Cuyjet's dance development.

Cuyjet was in her late 20s and had since discontinued her studies and teaching responsibilities with Dorsey when she entered the first stage of her commitment to a career as a dance educator. She began by offering ballet classes at home for her daughter and her friends. This venture served as a trial run for Cuyjet's future career aspirations. Its success encouraged her to enter a partnership with Sydney King. Thus began her second stage of commitment. Cuyjet possessed a solid support system for these initial experiences. The interest which was generated by her family, friends, and Dorsey contributed to her motivation and determined spirit. They understood Cuyjet's need to embrace a vocation in which she excelled.

Cuyjet's master plan for success included preparing herself as a proficient dance instructor. She first sought the assistance of Thomas Cannon. Her relationship with Cannon enabled her to meet and study with Nancy Lynch, another local dance educator. During the same time period, she studied at the William Sena School. Each of these teachers who were white, became Cuyjet's friend and advisor. Through her association with them, she discovered the importance of building a network of supporters in the field. She also retained from each teacher those aspects of their teaching approach which she deemed as successful teaching techniques. By the time she opened Judimar, her teaching methodology included elements from Dorsey, Cannon, Lynch, Sena, and teachers with whom she studied in New York.

Cuyjet entered the third stage of her independent teaching career by establishing the Judimar School of Dance. The school represented a vehicle for the transmission of Cuyjet's vision. She assembled an organization which would offer the finest dance preparation possible. She enlisted the aid of leading dance educators and dance accompanists in Black Philadelphia to insure high caliber training.

John Hines had an immense impact on Cuyjet's development as a teacher during her third stage of commitment. He gave her the incentive to take advantage of New York dance studios and introduced her to African-based dance forms through his knowledge of Dunham Technique. Hines initiated the Philadelphia-Dunham connection and Cuyjet joined him in promoting this emerging Africentric dance technique as an essential dance experience for dancers in Black Philadelphia. Hines and Cuyjet shared a trusting and loyal friendship and they were kindred souls throughout their respective careers.

Cuyjet's commitment to her vision became solidified during the 1950s. It was a period in American history when the struggle for equality for Black Americans began to gain momentum. The mainstream dance world's acceptance of African American dancers Janet Collins, Alvin Ailey, and Mary Hinkson inspired Cuyjet's vision. Collins's professional ballet debut was a symbol of hope for Black dancers who aspired to enter the ballet world. The prospect of desegregating the concert stage became a possibility. Cuyjet, however, was not preoccupied with challenging the entire mainstream concert dance culture. Her priority was making dance training available to youth in Black Philadelphia, regardless of their level of dance proficiency.

Cuyjet's personality distinguished her among her colleagues. She was assertive, goal-oriented, enthusiastic, courageous, energetic, and savvy. Her most dominant characteristic trait was her determined spirit. She applied strong doses of perseverance to sustain herself throughout her career, and her family played an integral role in both her personal and professional life. Their involvement in the administration of the Judimar School was instrumental in its success. Cuyjet was fortunate in being able to integrate her personal life with her vocation. Unlike some women in the dance field before the 1970s, she did not have to forego marriage and family in order to forge her career.

During the beginning of her career, Cuyjet's firm belief in her mission seemed to compensate for her novice teaching skills. Her strong conviction enabled her to convince Sydney King, who was most considered the "dancer," that they had something to offer the community. Cuyjet possessed self-motivation, and she had been influenced by Essie Marie Dorsey's tenacity and determination.

Delores Browne referred to Cuyjet as a "gutsy lady," because of her tendency to pursue ambitious production projects. She was constantly amazed that Cuyjet staged successful classical ballet pieces with student dancers and limited financial assistance. Colleague Joe Nash remarked on Cuyjet's infectious enthusiasm and energy. The zest with which she approached her work influenced everyone around her, and it was a key ingredient to the success of her school. Cuyjet's courageous, savvy attributes were exemplified when she dared desegregate an all-white business district in downtown Philadelphia by opening her first independent school at 1310 Walnut Street. Many of the landlords she rented from assumed that Cuyjet was white. She strategically used her fair skin as a means of obtaining leasing opportunities otherwise closed to African Americans. In addition, she was keenly aware of the importance of consulting her attorney when dealing with landlords who resisted extending her leasing terms. According to Cuyjet, she occasionally passed for white in order to open doors for her students. This often meant that other Black Philadelphians also benefited.

During her career, Cuyjet had to contend with several forces which tested her spirit. One of the most critical obstacles during the first decade of Judimar was securing permanent studio space. The average length of residence for the school's first four studios was one to two years. Most of the landlords complained about the noise and grew leery of renting to a predominately African American organization. Judimar's fifth residence, "the dance educators building" located on 2011 Chancellor Street, was secured for five years. The decision to rent the entire building and develop a dance institution based on a cooperative dance educators concept, proved to be a wise venture. John Hines, and Ann Bernadino Hughes, continued to teach for Cuyjet and they were given the opportunity to launch independent dance organizations. This collective economic and educational concept had a positive effect on the institution's longevity and popularity.

Throughout Judimar's existence, economic survival was a prime concern. Even when the school was in its heyday during the 1950s, tuition and the profits generated by the recitals and the Mothers Club were never enough to cover expenses on time. Regardless of the school's financial instability, Cuyjet always managed to provide free tuition for gifted students.

Cuyjet's precarious physical condition constantly challenged her determined spirit. A spinal problem caused by a fall down the cellar steps and a foot injury, the result of a fall she incurred while teaching class, caused considerable physical stress. Cuyjet coped with the spinal injury, yet neglected to curtail her strenuous teaching schedule. As a result, the condition steadily deteriorated. The foot injury finally persuaded Cuyjet to proceed with caution. Her relentless quest for building a tradition of excellence in dance education, regardless of her physical health, threatened her teaching endurance and caused the temporary demise of her teaching career in the early 1970s.

Cuyjet's most heartbreaking challenge was coping with the debilitating illness (Huntington's disease) of her husband. Stephen Cuyjet was Cuyjet's most ardent supporter and her business partner. He willingly embraced his wife's vision. His most important contribution was relieving Cuyjet of the intricacies of operating a business so that she could be free to teach and create dances. When his condition worsened during the late 1950s, Cuyjet moved the studio near their home. Cuyjet was now primary caretaker for her husband and Judimar. Stephen Cuyjet's passive involvement with Judimar, during the 1960s, left a void in the Judimar experience.

Cuyjet's visibility in the community by way of Christmas Cotillion collaborations, guest appearances with the Philadelphia Concert Orchestra, and the Dra Mu Opera Company, facilitated her popularity and influential standing in the cultural arts community. Her involvement with the New York dance studios and her affiliation with prominent dancer-educators such as Joe Nash, Ernest Parham, George Chaffee, and Luigi, undoubtedly impressed the local community. Cuyjet's friendship and professional relationship with Jay Dash, a dance educator in the larger Philadelphia community, allowed her to impact the white dance education community.

Cuyjet's consistent ability to produce proficient dancers like Browne, Warren, Jamison, and Ball in the 1950s, bolstered her influence. She proved that if African Americans were given an equal chance to receive authentic dance preparation, they could acquire a professional level of proficiency.

Cuyjet's popularity with middle-class Black Philadelphians was partly due to her affiliation with Dorsey, a Black socialite. Parents who considered themselves part of the Black elite gravitated to Cuyjet's school. The social class-stratification system based on length of residence in the city and skin color placed Cuyjet in the forefront of acceptability with a considerable amount of social clout.

Cuyjet's position as a part-time faculty member at Cheyney University of Pennsylvania, Delaware State University, and University of Maryland at Eastern Shore, distinguished her as the only dance educator in Black Philadelphia with experience in higher education as well as community educational environments. It was a rare occurrence that a studio-based dance educator received the opportunity to teach in a college or university setting. This accomplishment placed Cuyjet in a category all her own.

A final view of the circumstances surrounding Cuyjet's rise to one of Black Philadelphia's leading proponents of dance education will revolve around four characteristic aspects of her work: emphasis on excellence, educating the total person, commitment to artistic integrity, and promoting social change.

Cuyjet adhered to high standards in teaching, in the operation of her school, and in staging recital productions. Surpassing mediocrity was paramount. Cuyjet was best known for her reputation as an adept teacher and strict disciplinarian. In retrospect, many of her former students view her stern disposition in class as positive because her attitude influenced them to approach their studies in a serious vein.

Cuyjet's teaching approach stressed performance and an academic knowledge of the theory, craft, and history of ballet. She knew that proficiency in these areas would distinguish her students from the average dancer. According to former students who pursued professional careers, Cuyjet's teaching approach prepared them for a dance world in which African Americans had to be technically superior in order to achieve minimal success.

Cuyjet's attitude toward striving to be the "best" was shaped by her first dance teacher and mentor, Essie Marie Dorsey. According to Sydney King, Dorsey stressed the importance of aspiring for high achievement standards in their personal and dance lives. King states: "Dorsey told us that Black people had to be better" (personal communication, February 25, 1985). Her attitude was grounded in a silent belief held by many African Americans: to escape invisibility and achieve success in American society, one has to be excellent; good is not enough.

Cuyjet's emphasis on excellence was also grounded in a personal desire to become successful. She accepted her fate as an adequate dance technician, but was determined to develop as an exceptional dance educator. Her intense self-motivation gave her a positive vision of her capabilities.

Although Cuyjet founded the Judimar School of Dance to provide dance preparation, the school also functioned as an institution dedicated to the transmission of social, cultural, educational, and aesthetic values. Cuyjet was concerned with educating the whole person. She sponsored cultural outings during the summer school session, and social gatherings during the regular session. Because of her attitude toward formal education, she persistently reminded students of the importance of continuing their education after high school.

The homey atmosphere created by the involved presence of Cuyjet's immediate family gave the studio an environment conducive to a sense of community. The school supported an extended family orientation common to traditional African American communities.

Judimar's students cultivated an appreciation for European American aesthetic values through their concentrated involvement with ballet. In order to balance their cultural taste, Cuyjet exposed them to African-based dance forms. The result was a cultural experience that encouraged them to take caution with European American aesthetic assimilation and maintain an appreciation of their African heritage.

Cuyjet's commitment to artistic integrity permeated her work. She advocated aspiring to artistic standards established by the New City York professional dance community. She brought in dancers such as Joe Nash, Ernest Parham, and George Chaffe to Judimar, as role models and for artistic inspiration and direction. Her students were nurtured to be expressive communicators in the classroom and on the stage. They developed artistic sensibilities often associated with seasoned professionals.

The meticulous attention given to the development of recital pieces reflected Cuyjet's interest in the creative process. Developing scenarios and choreography, designing costumes, choosing the appropriate sets, lights, and music, were vital aspects of Judimar's recital preparation. Cuyjet's reputation as a fine technique teacher overshadowed her identity as a choreographer. Very few supporters outside the Judimar School were aware of her keen artistic intelligence used in the creation of cotillion and recital dance works.

Cuyjet was committed to nurturing brown-skinned ballerinas during an era in which Black dancers were excluded from the mainstream concert dance arena. She aspired to change the general public's attitude about the ability of Blacks to perform ballet technique on a professional level. She was also concerned with providing Black dancers the opportunity to change their own attitudes about their potential for successfully executing techniques outside of the realm of show dancing. Cuyjet's aspirations for her students were in the tradition of Katherine Dunham and Pearl Primus, dance pioneers who paved the way for the acceptance of Black dancers as concert dance artists.

The social change policies aimed at dismantling racial discrimination in the North during the 1950s had an impact on easing segregation in dance studios in New York. Cuyjet took advantage of the desegregation policies and enrolled her most gifted students. Each time she took her students to New York she exposed them to a predominately white population with preconceived ideas about the ballet aptitude of Blacks. Their exceptional performance in class proved that it is talent and training, not skin color, that make a ballet dancer.

Cuyjet's efforts toward social change in the Philadelphia dance community were manifested in the establishment of an interracial policy at her school. Judimar's open door policy was a vehicle for promoting cooperation between Black and white dancers. In the 1960s, Cuyjet's association with the Jay Dash dance studio, and her invitation to Joan Kerr to offer a Horton seminar at Judimar, further encouraged collaboration between Black and white dance education communities.

Cuyjet remained a leading proponent of dance education in Black Philadelphia for 23 years because of her dedication to offering quality dance preparation and her conviction that she could make a contribution to the quality of life in Black Philadelphia. Due to her involvement with community-wide cultural arts production and Judimar recitals, she helped foster a genuine appreciation of dance as an art form. She galvanized the performing arts community by lending her choreographic and production expertise. In addition, the Judimar School provided a supportive environment for the professional growth and development of musicians and dance educators. The school afforded them the opportunity to secure small-scale employment, artistic development, and to maintain visibility in the community. Most importantly, Judimar was an institution where youth could focus their creative energies in productive and meaningful ways.

Cuyjet's journey reveals that there was a thriving dance education community in Black Philadelphia from the late 1940s to the early 1970s. Dance students who were nurtured during that time period were fortunate to have been guided by dance educators who were unconditionally committed to developing proficient dance artists. Cuyjet emerged as a passionate and influential ballet pedagogue. She is responsible for mentoring future dance educators, performers, and choreographers, and through their work, her vision and legacy will impact dance in Philadelphia beyond the 20th century.

Postscript

In the late 1960s and early 1970s, some of Cuyjet's advanced students were accepted into newly desegregated schools and companies. Tawny Turner performed with the Philadelphia Civic Ballet and China White was selected as one of the charter members of the Philadelphia-based Pennsylvania Ballet Company. Founder and artistic director Arthur Mitchell, welcomed White as a principal dancer with the Dance Theatre of Harlem in New York City (see Plates 37 and 38) and she performed with the renowned ballet company from the early 1970s until 1980 (White-Dixon, 1995, p. 318). She maintains a successful dance studio (Theatre Street Dance Academy) and directs the pre-professional dance program at Fort Hayes Metropolitan Education Center in Columbus, Ohio. Former Judimar students, John Jones (Jerome Robbins' Ballet U.S.A. and Harkness Ballet) and Judith Jamison (Alvin Ailey American Dance Theatre), who succeeded in the New York City concert dance arena, also established impressive careers. Jones was a stunning dancer and in 1990 starred in the Gordon Parks ballet, *King,* which aired nationally on PBS television. Jamison is Marion Cuyjet's most well-known student, and in 1989 Alvin Ailey selected her to replace him as artistic director of the Alvin Ailey American Dance Theatre and the company thrived under her leadership and artistic vision (Dixon, 2004, p. 444).

After Cuyjet closed her school in 1971, she continued her interest in dance pedagogy by studying to be a movement therapist and served as a nurse's-aide and taught dance at Friends Hospital and at the Philadelphia State Hospital for eleven years. According to Philadelphia dance educator Doris Roberts, director of Philadelphia dance studio Soliloquy in Motion, Cuyjet often taught ballet for free at her home throughout the 1970s because of her passion for teaching and commitment to offering dance preparation for children without monetary means to pay for classes (personal communication, February 15, 2010). After her husband passed in 1980, Cuyjet continued to be an active member of Black Philadelphia's dance community. She taught for former student Cheryl Jenkins, director of La Cher Teri Dance School, and served as an advisor to Joan Myers Brown, director and founder of the Philadelphia School of Dance Arts (PSDA) and Philadanco. Her primary teaching activities revolved around children's pre-professional classes at PSDA and Philadanco company classes. Marion Cuyjet continued to teach until the early 1990s (see Plates 39 and 40).

According to primary contacts interviewed, the significance of Cuyjet's work was not recognized until after the Judimar School closed. After the Judimar era, she received numerous awards for her educational and artistic contributions to Black Philadelphia. She received accolades from Les Beaux Arts Cultural Society (mid-1970s), the Urban League (1982), Juba Contemporary Dance Company (1985), the Philadelphia Dance Company (1982), and Women's Way of Philadelphia (May 14, 1986).

April 1996, Cuyjet was a featured symposium speaker for the exhibit, "Classic Black, Photography Exhibit of African American Ballet Dancers," sponsored by the Dance Collection of the New York Public Library for the Performing Arts, and the Dance Research Foundation, New York City. The two videotaped public programs were significant events that allowed Cuyjet, former students and other pioneering African American colleagues including Doris Jones, Delores Browne, Louis Johnson, Betty Nichols, Raven Wilkinson, Joe Nash and Cleo Quitman, to tell their stories of perseverance and survival. The documentation project enabled Cuyjet and her contemporaries to receive long overdue public recognition for their contributions to the development of Black dancers in classical ballet (Greene, 1997, p. 86). Six months after her symposium appearance, "Miss Marion" passed October 22, 1996 at the age of 76. She was memorialized in the *Philadelphia Inquirer*, October 26, 1996, *New York Times*, October 27, 1996, during the Mass of Christian Burial, Saturday, November 2, 1996 at Saint Luke's Church, Philadelphia, Pennsylvania, and at the 1997 nationally televised NAACP Image Awards during its pictorial memorial presentation.

To honor her legacy, members of the Philadelphia dance community, including Joan Myers Brown, Delores Browne and Howard (Sid) Lucus, organized a memorial service in honor of Cuyjet, "A Celebration of a Life in Dance: In Remembrance of Marion Durham Cuyjet." The program was held at the University of the Arts Theatre in Philadelphia on November 14, 1996. There were remarks from family, former students, colleagues, and performances from selected dance companies and dancers from the Philadelphia's Black dance community. The video documentation of the event is housed at the Dance Collection of the New York Public Library for the Performing Arts.

As an everlasting testament to Cuyjet's contributions, Joan Myers Brown and Judith Cuyjet established the Marion D. Cuyjet Scholarship Fund and in 1997 its first recipient was Philadanco dancer Hollie Wright. Other recipients include Philadanco II dancer Iquail Shaheed and Alvin Ailey Dancer Abdur-Rahim Jackson.

Cuyjet's artistry and wisdom continues in the work of several dancers and dance educators who are active in Philadelphia. Although dance schools in the Philadelphia community are now open to all ethnicities, there still remains a strong African American dance school presence supported by teachers and dancers that are ramifications of Cuyjet's pedagogical legacy.

According to Doris Roberts, there are about 20 dance studios in Philadelphia whose teachers and directors can trace their roots back to Marion Cuyjet (personal communication February 10, 2010). Cuyjet's former colleague Sydney King, no longer teaching, continues to operate her dance studio at the age of 90 in West Philadelphia. With the support of family and former students, the studio has struggled yet survived through the challenges of West Philadelphia "Urban Renewal" projects. The longevity of The Sydney King School of Dance (6174 Market Street) is a source of pride for the neighboring community (John-Hall, 2009, n.p.).

Delores Browne, Cuyjet's first student to perform professionally, continues to teach company ballet class for Philadanco, and the dancers she nurtures will exemplify the Cuyjet training model in the twenty-first century. Joan Myers Brown, who relied on Cuyjet's prowess and advice in establishing her Philadelphia School of Dance Arts, has transformed her company, Philadanco, into a dance institution of national and international prominence. She is also the founder of the International Association of Blacks in Dance (IABD), a dance service organization that supports training, funding, and performance opportunities for dancers, dance educators, choreographers, and dance companies of the Black continuum in dance. Judith Jamison's leadership and artistic direction of the Alvin Ailey American Dance Theatre from 1989 to 2010 allowed Cuyjet's determined spirit and mission to be passed on to the most celebrated modern dance company in the world. Cuyjet's vision continues and her legacy is alive.

APPENDIX A

Definition of Terms and Glossary of Ballet Terms

Definition of Terms

The Cecchetti Method is a ballet technique developed by dancer, choreographer, and teacher Enrico Cecchetti (1850–1928). It is sometimes referred to as the Italian Method. The performing style stresses technical virtuosity and the class technique emphasizes a program of strict routine in practicing the five classical body positions and the seven categories of locomotor ballet movements. The method has influenced ballet training in Europe and America, specifically Italy, Russia, Great Britain, and the United States (Cohen-Stratyner, 1982, p. 186).

Dunham Technique was developed in the mid-1940s by dancer, choreographer, anthropologist, and African American dance pioneer Katherine Dunham (1914–2006). It is a combination of African and Afro-Caribbean dance with ballet and modern dance as additional components. It is the official technique of the Katherine Dunham Dance Company.

The ***French School*** refers to a system of ballet technique developed by French dance masters after the French Revolution. It is characterized by decorative arm and leg movements and emphasizes the charm and elegance of classical ballet. Like the Cecchetti Method, it is based on the five classical body positions and the seven kinds of classical ballet movements (Hammond, 1982, p. 38; and Kraus, 1969, p. 84).

Graham Technique is a system of modern dance training developed by dancer, choreographer, teacher, and modern dance pioneer Martha Graham (1893–1991). It emphasizes continuous unfolding movement from a central core, spasm and resistance, falls and recoveries from the floor, and contraction and release of the torso (Demille, 1963, p. 157).

Horton Technique was developed by dancer, choreographer, and teacher Leston Horton (1906–1953). It was the official modern dance technique of his West Coast dance school and company from 1934 to 1954. The technique evolved from Horton's choreographic and teaching experiences. It uses a long, stretched out body line, diagonal tension, and long balances which make the torso the center of everything that happens in the body. Leading exponents of Horton Technique are the late Alvin Ailey, Carmen de Lavallade, the late Joyce Trisler, the late James Truitte, and the late Bella Lewitsky (Mazo, 1977, p. 248).

Humphrey-Weidman refers to the artistic collaboration between modern dance pioneers Doris Humphrey (1895-1958) and Charles Weidman (1901-1975). The Humphrey-Weidman Company and school were divided into two systems of dance preparation, one structured (Humphrey's), and one intuitive (Weidman's). Humphrey was concerned with ordering space and time in a logical manner. She invented a codified modern dance style and technique. Weidman was concerned with action and character and his style was a blend of pantomime and dance (Mazo, 1977, p. 126).

Pointe work is dancing on the extreme tips of all toes of the foot (the arch of which is extended) with the aid of satin ballet slippers. The toe section of pointe shoes is hardened with layers of glue (Vaganova, 1969, p. 109).

Spanish Dance evolved and developed in the Iberian Peninsula. The choreography is of four distinct styles: regional (communal traditional folk dance), flamenco (originated by Gypsies and utilizing heel-work), school (stylized folk routines), and renaissance or neo-Spanish (old school dances set to the music of Iberian composers). A characteristic feature of Spanish dance is the proud and sensuous carriage of the head, torso, and arms (Chujoy & Manchester, 1967, pp. 855–857).

The Tiller System of precision-line dance training was developed by English dance teacher John Tiller (1852–1925). Tiller operated schools in London and Manchester. These studios trained dancers into eight, twelve, or sixteen-women precision teams using musical comedy or tap technique. By 1912, there were Tiller teams performing in Paris, Bordeaux, Australia, Austria, Turin, Glasglow, through England, and the United States. Tiller did not stage routines; he only trained performers (Cohen-Stratyner, 1982, p. 878).

The Vaganova School is the Soviet system of ballet education developed by teacher, dancer, Agrippina Vaganova (1879–1951). Characteristics of the system are emotional expressiveness, strictness of form, and a resolute, energetic manner of performance. Vaganova method aims at teaching pupils to "dance with their whole body [sic]," to acquire harmony of movements, and to widen their expressive range (Vaganova, 1969, pp. xi–xii).

Glossary of Ballet Terms.

The following definitions are based on information in the *Technical Manual and Dictionary of Classical Ballet* by Gail Grant.

Adagio. Adage is a French word derived from the Italian adagio meaning at ease or leisure. Adagio is a series of exercises following the center practice, consisting of a succession of slow and flowing movements.

Allegro. Brisk, lively. A term applied to all bright and brisk movements. It is used to refer to most elevation movements done in succession.

Arabesque. One of the basic poses in ballet, arabesque takes its name from a Moorish ornament. In ballet it is a position of the body, in profile, supported on one leg, which can be straight or demi-plié, with the other leg extended behind and at right angles to it.

Assemblé. Assembled or joined together. A step in which the working foot slides well along the ground before being swept into the air. As the foot goes into the air the dancer's body springs into the air also. To finish the movement both legs come to the ground simultaneously in fifth position.

Attitude. A particular pose in dancing derived by Carlo Blasis from the statue of Mercury by Giovanni da Bologna. It is a position on one leg with the other lifted in back, the knee bent at an angle of ninety degrees and well turned out so that the knee is higher than the foot. The supporting leg is on the floor.

Balancoire, en. Like a seesaw. Term applied to a leg kick when executed with a continuous swinging motion.

Battement. Beating. A beating action of the extended or bent leg.

Battu. Beaten. Any step embellished with a beat is called a pas battu.

Brisé. Broken breaking. A small beating step in which the movement is broken. Brisés are commenced on one or two feet and end on one or two feet.

Brisé volé. Flying brisé. In this brisé the dancer finishes on one foot after the beat, the other leg crosses either front or back.

Cambré. Arched. The body is bent from the waist, backward or sideways, the head following the movement of the body.

Chaînés. Chains, links. This is an abbreviation of the term "tours chaînés deboules": A series of rapid turns on the pointes, or demi-pointes done in a straight line or in a circle.

Changement. Change of the feet. Changements are spring steps in the fifth position, the dancer changing feet in the air and then landing in fifth position plié.

Chassé. Chased. A step in which one foot literally chases the other out of its position.

Coupé. Cut, cutting. A small intermediary step done as a preparation or impetus for some other step. It takes its name from the fact that one foot cuts the other away and takes its place.

Dedans, en. Inward. In steps and exercises the term en dedans indicates that the leg moves in a circular direction, counter clockwise from back to front.

Degagé. Disengaged. A degage is the pointing of the foot in an open position with a fully arched instep.

Dehors, en. Outward. In steps and exercises the term en dehors indicates that the leg moves in a circular direction, clockwise.

Demi-plié. Half bend of the knees. All steps of elevation begin and end with a demi-plié.

Echappé Escaping or slipping movement. An echappé is a level of opening of both feet from a closed to an open position. In each case echappés are done to the second or fourth position, both feet traveling an equal distance from the original center of gravity.

En Croix. In the shape of a cross. Indicates that an exercise is to be executed to the front, side, and back.

Entrechat. Interweaving or braiding. A step of beating in which the dancer jumps into the air and rapidly crosses the legs before and behind each other.

Flex. To bend. A movement that reduces the angle at a joint.

Fondu developpé. Fondu is a term to denote sinking down. Developpé means developed. Fondu developpé is a term used to describe a lowering of the body made by bending the knee of the supporting leg while the working leg is drawn up and slowly extended to an open position in the air and held there.

Frappé jeté, Frappé tendu. Frappé means to strike. Frappé jeté is a term used when the working foot beats the supporting leg at the neck of the foot then strikes the ball of the foot and rising several inches off the floor in a strong point. Frappé tendu is similar to frappé jeté except that after striking the floor the foot does not rise off the floor.

***Fouetté*.** Whipped. The sharp whipping around of the body from one direction to another.

***Glissade*.** Glide. A traveling step executed by gliding the working foot from the fifth position in the required direction, the other foot closing to it. It is used to link other steps, especially in allegro and across the floor combinations.

***Grande plié*.** The full bending of the knees where by the torso and pelvis of the body are lowered to the floor.

***Jeté, battement*.** Thrown and beaten. A jump from one leg to the other in which the working leg is brushed into the air and appears to be thrown. Before the dancer returns to the floor the working leg beats the supporting leg at the ankle.

***Pas de bourreé*.** Bourreé step. A series of quick little steps in place on full pointe or half pointe. The step is done alternating sides as rapidly as possible and remaining in place.

***Petit battement*.** A term which refers to foot movements that disengage, strike, stretch and lift.

***Piqué*.** Pricked, pricking. Executed by stepping directly on the pointe or demi-pointe of the working foot in any desired direction or position with the other foot raised in the air.

***Pirouette*.** Whirl or spin. A complete turn of the body on one foot either on the pointe or demi-pointe, the motive power being obtained from a combination of plie and arm movement.

***Porte de bras*.** Carriage of the arms. A movement or series of movements made by passing the arm or arms through various positions.

***Porte en l'air*.** Carried in the air. This term refers to a step which is traveled in the air from one spot to another.

***Positions of the feet (five)*.** There are five basic positions of the feet in classical ballet and every step or movement is begun and finished in one or another of these positions. First position—The feet from a 120 to 180 degree angle with both heels touching. Second position—The feet form the same angle but with a distance of about one foot between the heels. Third position—In the third position one foot is in front of the other, heel touching the middle of the other foot. Fourth position—This position is similar to that in the third position, the feet being parallel and separated by the length of one foot. Fifth position—The feet are crossed so that the heel of the front foot touches the toe of the back foot and vice versa.

Relevé. Raised. A raising of the body on the pointes or demi-pointes.

Retiré. Withdrawn. A position in which the thigh is raised to the second position en l'air so that the toe is in line with and touching the knee of the supporting leg either front or back.

Reverence. Reverence, curtsy. The elaborate curtsy and bow performed by the dancers to acknowledge the applause of the audience.

Ronde de Jambe. Circling of the leg. A grande ronde de jambe is a large circling of the leg. Ronde de jambe a terre is performed on the floor and ronde de jambe en l'air is executed in the air.

Sur le cou-de-pied. On the neck of the foot. It is the position of one foot placed on the ankle of the other foot so that the heel protrudes in front of the supporting leg. The knee of the raised foot is turned outward toward second position.

Sous-sus. Under-over. Sous-sus is a relevé in the fifth position traveled forward, backward, or to the side. The dancer springs onto the pointes, drawing the legs and feet tightly together.

Tendu battement. Battement stretched. A tendu is the commencing portion and ending portion of a grande battement and is an exercise to force the insteps well outward. The foot slides to a pointe on the floor.

Tour de basque. Basque turn. Execute a demi route de jambe en l'air outwards, then step up on the right foot with the other foot open to second position. Take the left foot and whip it inward to turn the body inward a full turn.

Tour jeté. Large jeté over and turning. This is similar to the leap (grande jeté) except that in mid-air the body is flung over (turning inward) to face the direction from which the jump originated and landing in demi-plié in an arabesque position.

Tour en l'air. Turn in the air. It is a turn in which the dancer makes a complete turn in the air then lands in fifth position.

APPENDIX B

Listing of Selected Former Judimar Students

Judith Cuyet

TIME PERIOD AT JUDIMAR: 1948–1959

AREA OF CONCENTRATION: Ballet; dancer-teacher-choreographer

PROFESSIONAL ACTIVITIES AND ACHIEVEMENTS:

- Performed with Philadelphia Civic Ballet, Capital Ballet, Washington, D.C. (1960s)
- Received B.A. in Physical Education/English Minor, Maryland State University
- Graduate studies at Howard University and George Washington University
- Physical Education teacher and ballet instructor, White Oak Jr. High, Silver Springs, MD. (1962–1971)
- Director of Young Peoples Dance Theatre, Pullman, Washington (1971–1974)
- Choreographed for Judimar, Faye Snow Dance Co., Philadelphia (late 1970s)
- English teacher for Cherokee High School, Marton, New Jersey (1975–2003)

Gail Nelson

TIME PERIOD AT JUDIMAR: 1957–1959

AREA OF CONCENTRATION: Musical Theater

PROFESSIONAL ACTIVITIES AND ACHIEVEMENTS:

- B.A. in Music, Oberlin College (1960s), Oberlin, Ohio

- Performed in *Hallelujah Baby, Lost in the Stars* (Off Broadway), *Hello Dolly* (Summer Stock–Late 1960s) *Eubie* (Broadway—1975), *Bubbling Brown Sugar* (Broadway Road Shows 1982–86), *Tap Dance Kid* (Broadway 1985 and 1986)
- Sang with Opera Studio School of the Metropolitan Opera Co., NYC. (late 1960s, The Vienna Chamber Opera (1969)
- NYC. night club circuit and Musical theatre including "Lady Day: At Emerson's Bar and Grill" (1980s to the present)

China White

TIME PERIOD AT JUDIMAR: 1959–1963

AREA OF CONCENTRATION: Ballet; dancer-teacher

PROFESSIONAL ACTIVITIES AND ACHIEVEMENTS:

- Original member of Pennsylvania Ballet Co., Phila. (1963)
- Received B.S. in Physical Education from Ohio State University (1969)
- Performed with Dance Theatre of Harlem (1971 to 1980, Principal dancer)
- Performed in the Film the Wiz (1978)
- Received M.A. in Dance from Ohio State University (1984)
- Founder and Director of Theatre Street Dance Academy and dance instructor at Fort Hayes High School, Columbus, Ohio (1985 to present)

John Jones

TIME PERIOD AT JUDIMAR: 1951–1955

AREA OF CONCENTRATION: Ballet

PROFESSIONAL ACTIVITIES AND ACHIEVEMENTS:

- Performed with Jerome Robbins Ballet USA (1958–1961), Harkness Ballet (1965–1967), Dance Theatre of Harlem (early 1970s), American Dance Machine (early to mid-1970s) Choreographed for American Dance Machine, Pennsylvania Ballet, Alvin Ailey American Dance Theatre (early to mid-1970s)
- Taught for Judimar (1960s), Philadelphia School of the Performing Arts (early to mid-1970s)

- Director and founder of Dance Theatre-USA (United Souls of America, Philadelphia (early 1970s), Artistic Director and teacher for Arthur Hall Afro-American Dance Ensemble (1973)
- Dance teacher in Tokyo, Japan, (mid to late 1970s)
- Guest artist and teacher-Rod Rodgers Dance Company, New York City (1986–1990s)
- Lead dancer for Gordon Parks' ballet *King* (1990)

Cheryl Jenkins

TIME PERIOD AT JUDIMAR: 1956–1959

AREA OF CONCENTRATION: Ballet; dancer-teacher

PROFESSIONAL ACTIVITIES AND ACHIEVEMENTS:

- Founder and director of Philadelpiha studio, La Cher Teri (late 1980s)

Myrna Amai Munchus Bullock

TIME PERIOD AT JUDIMAR: 1956–1964

AREA OF CONCENTRATION: Ballet, Modern; dancer-teacher

PROFESSIONAL ACTIVITIES AND ACHIEVEMENTS:

- Performed with Phila. Civic Ballet (1964–1965), Dance Theatre U.S. of A. (mid-1970s), Frank Holder Dance Company, Greensboro, N.C. (1979–1980)
- Co-director and founder of Afro-One Dance Co., Willingboro, N.J., MFA and instructor Temple University (1983 to present)
- Director of Healing Hearts Sanctuary, Creative Arts and Psycho-Spiritual Healing (at present)

Helen Riley

TIME PERIOD AT JUDIMAR: mid-1950s to early 1960s

AREA OF CONCENTRATION: Ballet, Modern, Jazz, Afro-Caribbean, and African Dance forms; dancer-teacher

PROFESSIONAL ACTIVITIES AND ACHIEVEMENTS:

- Performed with the James Brown Revue (mid-1960s) Arthur Hall African American Dance Ensemble (late 1960s to early 1970s)
- Received M.A. in Dance Temple University (1985)
- Dance Specialist for the Harrisburg, Pa. school system (1980s)

Janice Harrison Fullard

TIME PERIOD AT JUDIMAR: mid to late 1960s

AREA OF CONCENTRATION: Ballet, Modern; dancer-actress

PROFESSIONAL ACTIVITIES AND ACHIEVEMENTS:

- Performed with Philadanco (early 1970s), Lena Horne (road show, 1983–85)
- Principal actress with Avante Theatre Co., Philadelphia (late 1980s)

Tamara Guillebeaux

TIME PERIOD AT JUDIMAR: late 1950s to mid-1960s

AREA OF CONCENTRATION: Ballet, Modern; dancer-teacher

PROFESSIONAL ACTIVITIES AND ACHIEVEMENTS:

- B.A. in dance (ballet) from Butler University, Indiana (late 1960s)
- Performed with Rod Rodgers Dance Company (early 1970s to early 1980s)
- Received M.A. in Dance from New York University (1976)

Pat Scott-Hobbs

TIME PERIOD AT JUDIMAR: late 1960s to early 1970s

AREA OF CONCENTRATION: Ballet, Modern, Jazz; dancer-teacher-choreographer

PROFESSIONAL ACTIVITIES AND ACHIEVEMENTS:

- B.A. in Dance, Temple University (early 1970s)
- Director of the Dance Dept. and Performing Arts Training Program Freedom Theatre, Philadelphia (1985–present)

Tawny Turner

TIME PERIOD AT JUDIMAR: late 1950s to 1971

AREA OF CONCENTRATION: Ballet; dancer-teacher

PROFESSIONAL ACTIVITIES AND ACHIEVEMENTS:

- Performed with Philadelphia Civic Ballet Co. (1971–1974)
- Taught for Peter Kodell Dance Studio, Philadelphia (mid-1970s), Tri-State Ballet Co. Upper Darby, Pa. (late 1970s)
- Dance instructor for the Ardmore, Pa. Dept. of Recreation (late 1970s to 1980s)

Charles Moore

TIME PERIOD AT JUDIMAR: early 1950s to mid 1950s

AREA OF CONCENTRATION: Ballet, Afro-Caribbean; dancer

PROFESSIONAL ACTIVITIES AND ACHIEVEMENTS:

- Dancer for Warner Bros. movie studio (mid-1950s to late 1950s)

Ronald Platts

TIME PERIOD AT JUDIMAR: early 1950s to mid 1950s

AREA OF CONCENTRATION: Ballet; dancer-teacher

PROFESSIONAL ACTIVITIES AND ACHIEVEMENTS:

- Performed with the companies of Alvin Ailey and Ernest Parham (late 1950s), the Merry-Go-Rounders (late 1950s), Kwamina (On-Brooadway 1961), Showboat (Off-Broadway revival at City Center 1961)
- Founder and director of private studio in Sweden (1960s to 1980s)

Rodney Green

TIME PERIOD AT JUDIMAR: late 1960s to 1971

AREA OF CONCENTRATION: Ballet, Modern; dancer-teacher

PROFESSIONAL ACTIVITIES AND ACHIEVEMENTS:

- Performed with Philadelphia Civic Ballet (1970), *The Wiz* (Broadway early 1970s), *Timbuktu* (Broadway-1978)
- Taught for Judimar (1970–71)

APPENDIX C

Marion D. Cuyjet's Resumé (1970)

RESUME OF:	Marion Helene Durham Cuyjet
ADDRESS:	1014 South 58th Street, Philadelphia, Pennsylvania, 19143
RES. PHONE:	Sh.18 6063
BUS. ADDRESS:	944 South 58th Street, Philadelphia, Pennsylvania 19143
BORN:	July 29, 1920, Philadelphia, Pennsylvania
MARRIED:	Stephen L. Cuyjet – (Living)

PUBLIC SCHOOLS:

Landreth Elementary School	(1932)
Barrett Junior High School	(1934)
South Phila. High School for Girls	(1937)

PROFESSIONAL SCHOOLS:

Philadelphia Office Training	(1938)

INCLUDED IN THIS RESUME:

Professional Dance Training and Affiliated Courses
Background Experiences
Lectures and Demonstrations
Teaching Experiences
Member Organizations
Affiliations - Past and Present

PROFESSIONAL DANCE TRAINING AND AFFILIATED COURSES

Essie Marie Dorsey School of Dance, Philadelphia, Pennsylvania

Scholarship 1934 to 1936 Student Teacher

1937 to 1939 Assistant Teacher

1939 to 1940 Ballet (Cecchetti Tech.) Tap and acrobatics

Philadelphia Ballet Co. (Catherine Littlefield) 1936–1938

Ballet (Russian Tech.) and Ballet terminology

Nance Lynch (Dance Instr.—Temple University) 1945–46

Kinesthetic and folk dancing

Katherine Dunham School of Theatre Arts, New York City

3 summer school sessions 1946–1948

Afro-Caribbean Primitive Dance Techniques, Modern dance—Jose Limon

Authentic Drum Rhythms of Africa and Virgin Isles

Anthropological Parallels in Dance

William Sena Ballet School 1948

Ballet Arts School (Carnegie Hall, New York City)

Summer Sessions 1950–1957

Instructors: Vladimir Dokoudovsky, Vera Nemtchinova, and Lisan Kay

George Chaffee, Maitre de Ballet, New York City

(Ballet Iconographer, collection permanent at Yale Univ.)

Ballet and Pedagogy (French and Russian Tech.)

History of the Dance

Summer and winter sessions 1950–1968

June Taylor School of Dance, New York City

Summer School Sessions 1957–1964

American and Modern Jazz techniques

Tiller line Group System Course Tap

Luigi (Hollywood and Broadway Musical) Choreographer

Summer sessions and weekly winter classes 1957–1960

Modern Jazz Styles and Tech. 1957–

Matt Mattox (Hollywood and Broadway Musicals and television Choreographer) Modern Jazz Styles and Tech. 1957–

Rhoda Winter Russell - Techniques of Movement Therapy

Course—Temple University, Philadelphia, Pennsylvania Field Work - Philadelphia State Hospital and Friends Hospital 1970

TEACHER:

1946–48 Opened business in partnership with Sydney King as the *Sydney-Marion School of Dance*

1948–1971 Owned and operated *The Judimar School of Dance* — registered under fictitious names Act, September 21, 1948, Court of Common Pleas #6, Philadelphia, Pennsylvania

During the 23 years between 1948 and 1971, instructed and choreographed for the following schools, colleges and organizations in addition to conducting classes and directing the *Judimar School* 1948–1949 *Wharton Center*, Philadelphia Recreation Department *Germantown Y.W.C.A.*

1949–1950 *Yeadon Community Center*, Yeadon, Pennsylvania

1951– *Judimar's School* increased enrollment necessitated enlarging the facilities, staff and classes. The undersigned excluded outside professional activities to install a training program for student teachers. Maternity, also, was included at this time.

1954–1967 Re-founded the *Essie Marie Dance Clinic*—headed staff for Essie Marie Dorsey (December-June 1967)

1958–1971 *Jay Dash Convention for Dance Teachers and Students* (Adelphia Hotel, Philadelphia, Pennsylvania) Director and instructor of Ballet and Modern Jazz courses—classes 9 a.m.–5 p.m., last week of July with published notes of routines and techniques.

1957–1969 *Maryland State College,* Princess Anne (division -University of Maryland) Dance Consultant and Collegiate Productions - also Community Dance classes -(Judimar Enterprise)

1958–1959 History of Dance—Physical Education Women (College Special Program)

1962–1963 Intra-Mural Dance for Women (College Special Program)

1963–1964 Rhythms Analysis Course—Physical Ed. Freshman Majors—3 hours accredited course. Women's physical Ed. Minors course—Modern Dance for Sophomores and Freshmen.—(substitute Phys. Ed. instructor—Univ. of Maryland.

1966–1969 "Upward Bound" program at Maryland State College, 4 summer sessions, each session—6 weeks

1958–1960 *Delaware State College*, Dover Delaware— Campus Kindergarten dance class, 11 a.m., Tuesday.—Phys. Ed. Dance Classes 2 and 3 p.m. Tuesdays.—Intra-Mural Dance Class 7 p.m. Tuesday.

1958–1960	*Cheyney State College*, Cheyney, Pennsylvania—Cheyney Modern Dance Group, 3 p.m., Thursdays.
1958–1967	*Jay Dash School of Dance*, 120 South 13th Street, Pennsylvania, Guest instructor, Ballet and Modern Jazz, 6:30 p.m. and 7:30 p.m. Weds.
1959	*Seminar and Workshop Instructor* Salisbury, Maryland Modern dance techniques of axial motivations
1962	*In-Service Course for Philadelphia Recreation Dept.* Modern dance: Teaching techniques and routines for non-dancers. Ten-week course for Dept. leaders and Public School Teachers.
1966–1967	*Alain Locke Elementary School Community Program* Instructor Classical Ballet for Children, Saturdays 9 a.m. - 11 a.m.
1967–1969	*Peter Kodel School of Dance,* 120 South 13th Street Philadelphia, Pennsylvania. Guest Instructor of Modern Dance 7:30 p.m. Wednesdays
1970	*Friends Hospital*, Philadelphia, Pennsylvania Employed full time as Nurse's Aide, purposefully to observe and study behavior of mental patients and general effects of psycho-pharmacology insofar as general body movement is concerned. *Volunteer Service*, conducts Movement and Dance Therapy sessions. (Friends Hospital does not employ this type of therapist.)

BACKGROUND INFORMATION:

1946–1947	2 Dance Recitals for Sydney-Marion School (Marion Cuyjet, partner)
1948–1971	23rd Annual Performances produced for the Judimar School of Dance (owned and operated by Marion D. Cuyjet)
1949–1964	13 Ballet presentations for Christmas Cotillion Society, Heritage house. Performance held at Convention Hall and the Academy of Music, Philadelphia, Pennsylvania
1952	Choreographer - Dra-Mu Opera Company's "Carmen" (Academy of Music)
1954	Seminar Teacher - National Association Dance and Affiliated Artists
1954	Choreographer - Dra-Mu Opera Company's - "Samson et Delila" Academy of Music
1956	Choreographer - National Negro Opera Company's "Aida" performed with the Pittsburgh Symphony at Syria Mosque, Pittsburgh, Pennsylvania
1957	Judimar Production at Maryland State College
1957	Produced "Caribbean Capers" - collegiate musical Maryland State College
1957	Television Dance Program - station WBOC, Salisburgy, Maryland
1957	Produced ballet for Buffalo Cotillion Society Buffalo, new York.

1958	Produced "Carmen Co-ed" (Bizet), collegiate production for Maryland State College
1958	Judimar Dance Concert at Maryland State and Delaware State Colleges.
1959	Delaware State College Student Recital
1959	Produced May Day presentation for Cheyney State College
1959	Judimar Dance Concert sponsored by Alpha Kappa Alpha Sorority at Dover, Delaware
1960–1961	"Amahl and the Night Visitors" — (Menotti) Company Co-produced Opera for Maryland State College music majors and dance group—2 annual performances
1962	Seminar teacher for Philadelphia Teachers Association, Dance Masters of America, Bellevue Stratford Hotel
1963	Philadelphia Board of Education TV Program, "Wiffil Schoolhouse" ~ station WFIL, 4 ballet excerpts and interviews
1965	Concert: Choreographed "Persephone at Pluto" 3 performances at Plays and Players, Delancey Street Philadelphia, Penna.
	Bucks County Ballet Co. - choreographed "Francesca da Rimini," (Tchaikovsky) for repertory performance at Bucks County Playhouse, New Hope, Pennsylvania

1968	Produced musical show for Maryland State College. Choir, band and dance groups - "Go Now, Pay Later" -funded by Wye Institute of Maryland - Production toured state.
1969	December—TV performance—"Blackboard" Christmas program WFIL-TV
1969	July—Produced TV program for Maryland State College; "Cultural Arts from the College to Community"

LECTURES:

1949	Philadelphia Tribune Newspaper's Cultural Forum: Topic: "History of Ballet and the Negro Professional Possibilities in that field."
1958	Delaware State College—"Delaware's Forgotten Folk" (The Moors) and the Role of the College

LECTURES AND DEMONSTRATIONS: PHILADELPHIA, PENNSYLVANIA

Fitzsimons Jr. High School
Barrett Jr. High School
Shoemaker Jr. High School
Roosevelt Jr. High School
Sulzberger Jr. High School
Wanamaker Jr. High School
Anderson Elem. School
Landreth Elem. School
Martha Wash. Elem. School
Alain Locke Elem. School
Blaine Elem. School
Douglass Singerly
Elementary School
Drew Elem. School
Dunbar Elem. School
McMichael Elem.School
Meade Elem. School
Reynolds Elem. School
St. Anthony's Parish School

OUT OF STATE

William Henry High School, Dover, Delaware

Moten High School, Easton, Maryland

Worchester High School, Snow Hill, Maryland

Maryland State College, Princess Anne, Maryland

Delaware State College, Dover, Delaware

Cheyney State College, Cheyney, Pennsylvania

Numerous performances for churches, sororities, fraternities, orphanages

Co-author of "The Primitive Dance" in 1950 edition of "Music and Dance" in Pennsylvania. Editor: Sigmund C. Spaeth

MEMBER ORGANIZATIONS

National Association Dance and Affiliated Artists
Pennsylvania Association of Teachers Association
American Dance Companies American Dance Teachers
Association Les Beaux Arts

AFFILIATIONS PAST AND PRESENT

Philadelphia Cotillion Society, Heritage House - Artistic

1949–1964 Production Consultant - Choreographer

1958–1962 Jay Dash School of Dance - Instructor-Choreographer
Jay Dash Dance Teachers Annual Dance Convention
Director of ballet and modern jazz courses

1967–1969 Peter Kodel School of Dance - Instructor and Choreographer

1957–1970	Maryland State College, Princess Anne - 13 years Visiting Lecturer and Dance Consultant, Dance Instructor: Physical Education Dept. and Intra-Mural program. Director: Community dance classes for children, teens and adults. Producer of student musicals and operetta
1958–1960	Cheyney State College - Cheyney, Pennsylvania
1958–1960	Delaware State College, Dover - Visiting lecturer and dance instructor for physical education dept., campus kindergarten and intra-mural program
1958–1960	Bucks County Ballet Company - Member board of Choreographer of "Francesca da Rimini" (Tchaikovsky) for company concert repertory.
1970	Church Lane Montessori School—Nursery and Kindergarten School—Director and instructor of pre-school dance techniques

Example of Judimar Summer Day School Announcement

The Judimar School of Dance Summer Day School

June 27th through August 6th

10 A.M. to 2 P.M. Daily

Beginner and Intermediate Students

Tuition Rates

Five Days per week (15 lessons) $13.50 per week
Three Days per week (9 lessons) $9.50 per week
Two Days per week (6 lessons) $6.50 per week

Advanced Students – Evening School
(6 P.M. to 9 P.M.)

Tuition Rates

6 Lessons for $12.00
10 Lessons for $18.00
12 Lessons for $22.00
18 Lessons for $31.00

Single Lesson Rates for Children in the Day School
Apply the Above "Evening School" Rates

Fall Registration
September 6th to 16th 1966
Judimar School of Dance
1014 South 58th Street

Plate 1. Marion Cuyjet circa 1950. Photograph by Gaston DeVigne Studio, Philadelphia, Pa. Reproduced through the courtesy of the Marion D. Cuyjet Private Collection.

Plate 2. Essie Marie Dorsey circa 1930. Photograph reproduced through the courtesy of the Marion D. Cuyjet Private Collection.

Plate 3. Stephen Lane Cuyjet Sr. United States Army portrait, circa 1944. Photograph by G. M. Wilson, Philadelphia, Pa. Reproduced through the courtesy of the Marion D. Cuyjet Private Collection.

Plate 4. Sydney G. King and Marion D. Cuyjet receiving flowers from their mentor Essie Marie Dorsey after the first recital of the Sydney-Marion School of Dance, circa 1947. Photograph by Gaston DeVigne Studio, Philadelphia, Pa. Reproduced through the courtesy of the Marion D. Cuyjet Private Collection.

Plate 5. Marion Cuyjet in a Dunham inspired costume from a 4th of July Philadelphia Fairmount Park performance for the Pheasant Club, circa 1948. Photograph by Gaston DeVigne Studio, Philadelphia. Pa. Reproduced through the courtesy of the Marion D. Cuyjet Private Collection.

DUNHAM TECHNIQUE FOR PHILADELPHIA

The Sydney-Marion School of Dance

is proud to announce that

SYVILLA FORT

head of the Dance Division of the Katherine Dunham School of Cultural Arts will be

GUEST TEACHER

at the Sydney-Marion Studio for a Special Course in Dunham Technique

Miss Syvilla Fort

(Dunham Technique-Primitive Rhythms-Ballet)

Graduate, U. of Washington and Cornish School of Theatre Arts. Featured dancer with Katherine Dunham Company for five years. Instructor, Experimental Dance at Martha Washington School for Girls.

Mr. Antoine Brevant

of the Pan-American Union says:

After witnessing the Dunham Experimental Dance Group at Howard University, June 26, 1947—"The Haitians' appreciate the cultural contribution of your school to a better interpretation and understanding of the Haitian background by the reproduction of those picturesque songs and dances which constitute undoubtedly apart of our common heritage."

REGISTRATION: MONDAY, AUG. 4th, 11th, 18th

Classes held Monday Evenings, 8 to 9 p. m.

CALL OR WRITE

SYDNEY-MARION SCHOOL OF DANCE

711 S. Broad St. KI 5-6281

Plate 6. Sydney-Marion School of Dance Flyer announcing Syvilla Fort Dunham Technique workshops, circa 1946. Reproduced through the courtesy of the Marion D. Cuyjet Private Collection.

Plate 7. Marion Cuyjet in publicity portrait, circa 1948. Photograph reproduced through the courtesy of the Marion D. Cuyjet Private Collection.

Plate 8. Philadelphia Christmas Cotillion debutante circle, circa 1950. Reproduced through the courtesy of the John W. Mosley Photographic Collections, Charles L. Blockson Afro-American Collection, Temple University Libraries, Philadelphia, Pa.

Plate 9. Actress Joan Crawford Steele receives the Philadelphia Cotillion Society *Cross of Malta* award. L-R: Judge Raymond Pace Alexander, Judimar student Donna Lowe (age 17), Mayor Richardson Dilworth, circa 1958. Photograph by Reuben E. Hall. Reproduced through the courtesy of the Marion D. Cuyet Private Collection.

Plate 10. L-R: Marion Cuyjet, Dr. Eugene Waymon Jones (center), and Sydney King (second from right) at the Philadelphia Christmas Cotillion Society Ball, circa 1953. Reproduced through the courtesy of the John w. Mosley Photographic Collection, Charles L. Blockson Afro-American Collection, Temple University Libraries, Philadelphia, Pa.

Plate 11. Marion Cuyjet and Sydney King accepting a recognition certificate from the University of Pennsylvania Cultural Olympics, circa 1948. Reproduced through the courtesy of the Marion D. Cuyjet Private Collection.

Plate 12. Billy Wilson partners his then wife Sonja Van Beers, for a television show in the Netherlands, circa, 1967. Photograph reproduced through the courtesy of the Billy Wilson Collection.

Plate 13. Joan Myers Brown in a Philadelphia School of Dance Arts publicity photo, circa 1960. Photograph reproduced through the courtesy of the Marion D. Cuyjet Private Collection.

Plate 14. Judimar Dance Company (experimental dance group). Ione Nash, left front on knees, back row standing L-R: Arthur Hall, George Williams, John Jones, and John Caruthers, circa 1950. Photograph reproduced through the courtesy of the Marion D. Cuyjet Private Collection.

Plate 15. Marion Cuyjet's parents Frances Henrietta Morgan Durham and Alonzo Durham, circa 1930. Photograph reproduced through the Courtesy of the Marion D. Cuyjet Private Collection.

Plate 16. Joe Nash performing *L'Afrique* at the Judimar School of Dance, circa 1953. Photographed reproduced through the courtesy of the Marion D. Cuyjet Private Collection.

Plate 17. First staff of the Judimar School of Dance. L-R: first row, Marion Cuyjet and Franca Jimenez, back row, Terez Nelson, John Hines, and Shirley Elsey, circa 1948. Photograph by Gaston DeVigne Studio, Philadelphia, Pa. Reproduced through the courtesy of the Marion D. Cuyjet Private Collection.

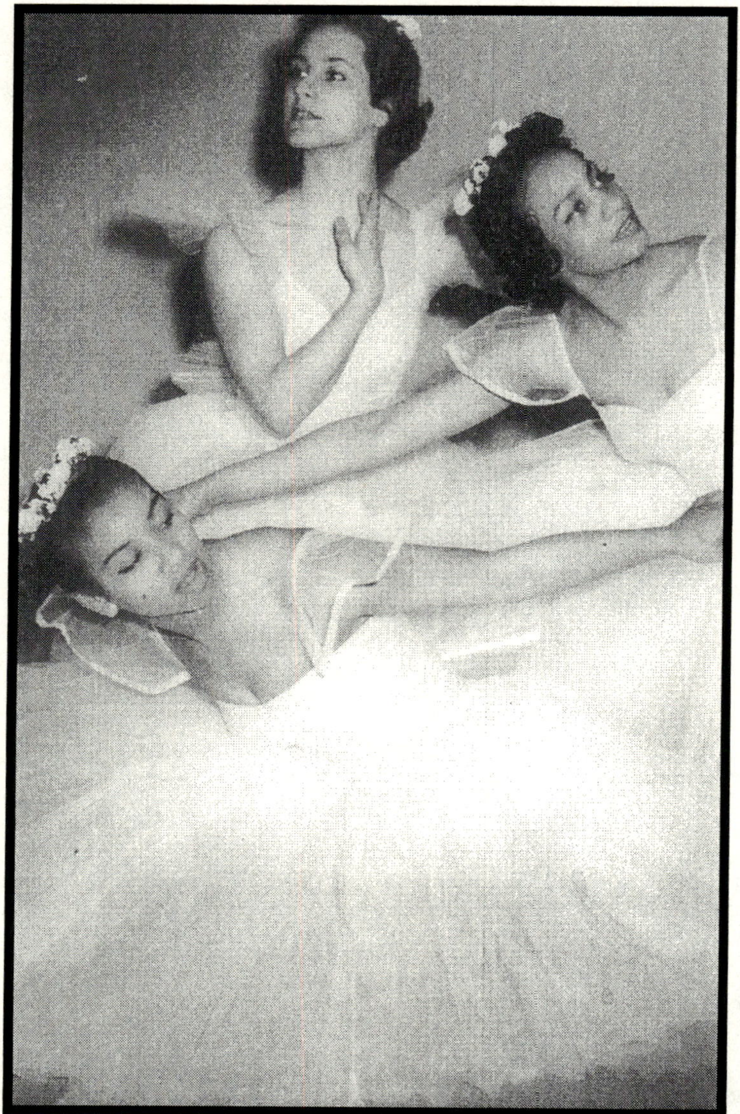

Plate 18. Judimar School of Dance recital performance. Front: Delores Browne, Middle: Franca Jimenez, Back: Judy Cuyjet, circa 1954. Photograph by Gi Ji, Philadelphia, Pa. Reproduced through the courtesy of the Marion D. Cuyjet Private Collection.

Plate 19. Bon Voyage party for Ernest Leigh Parham. L-R: Bottom Row, Yvonne Green, Franca Jimenez, Bobby Crowder, Delores Browne, Garvin Masseaux, Ronald Platts (behind Masseaux) Middle Row, Terez Nelson and husband, Judy Cuyjet, John Jones (behind Judy Cuyjet) Marie Jimenez McLeod, Ernie Parham, Marion Cuyjet, Charles Moore (behind Cuyjet), Samuel Caruthers, Joan Jackson. Top Row, Charles Medley, George Williams, Arthur Hall, and McCoy Tyner, circa 1953. Photograph reproduced through the courtesy of the Marion D. Cuyjet Private Collection.

Plate 20. Judimar School of Dance first recital performance, circa 1948. Photograph by Gaston DeVigne Studio, Philadelphia, Pa. Reproduced through the courtesy of the Marion D. Cuyjet Private Collection.

Plate 21. Marion Cuyjet with first scholarship students Alice Mays (Hall) and Juanita Jones (Fagan), circa 1949. Photograph reproduced through the courtesy of the Marion D. Cuyjet Private Collection.

Plate 22. Alice Mays and Juanita Jones performing in *Carmen* for a Judimar School of Dance recital, circa 1951. Photograph by Wert S. Hooper, Philadelphia, Pa. Reproduced through the courtesy of the Marion D. Cuyjet Private Collection.

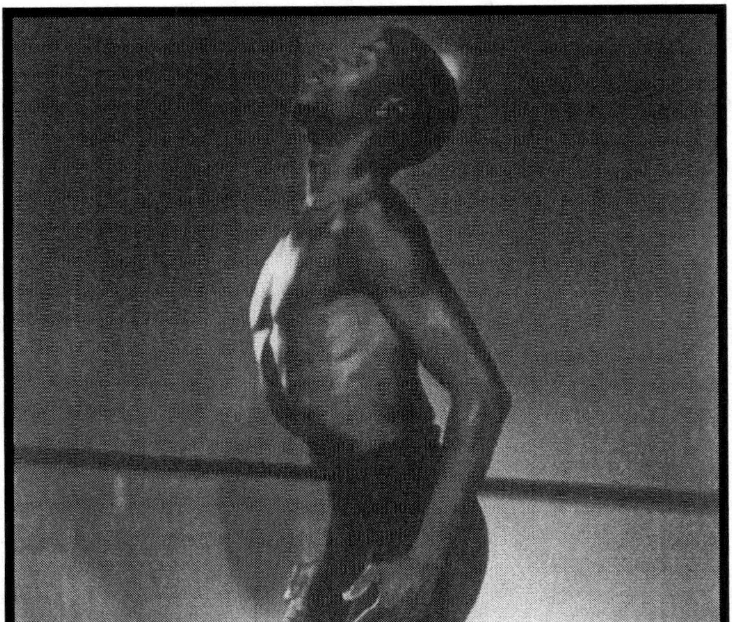

Plate 23. John Jones performing in London, circa 1960. Photograph by Anthony Crickmay. Reproduced through the courtesy of the Marion D. Cuyjet Private Collection.

Plate 24. Alice Mays, Delores Browne, and Juanita Jones performing in a Judimar School of Dance recital performance, circa 1953. Reproduced through the courtesy of the John W. Mosley Photographic Collection, Charles L. Blockson Afro-American Collection, Temple University Libraries, Philadelphia, Pa.

Plate 25. Judy Cuyjet as *Cinderella* in a Judimar School recital, circa 1950.
Photograph reproduced through the courtesy of the Marion D. Cuyjet Private Collection.

Plate 26. Joyce Graves in a Judimar School of Dance recital, circa 1955. Photograph reproduced through the courtesy of the Marion D. Cuyjet Private Collection.

Plate 27. Judimar Dance Company performs ballet excerpts for television program. L-R: unidentified dancer, Sally Richardson, Barbara Bullock, Donna Lowe, host of show, Marion Cuyjet, Joyce Graves and China White, circa 1957.
Photograph reproduced through the courtesy of the Marion D. Cuyjet Private Collection.

Plate 28. Delores Browne performing in *Carmen* for the Dru Mu Opera Company, circa 1951. Photograph reproduced through the courtesy of Marion D. Cuyjet Private Collection.

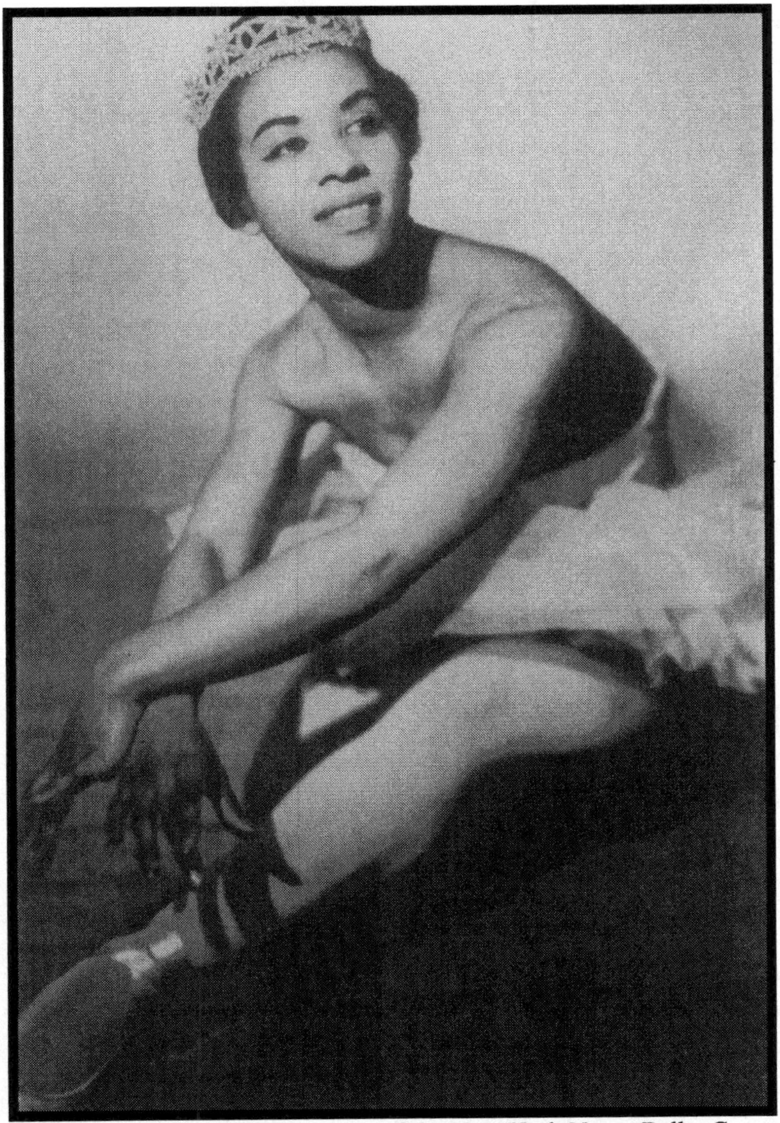

Plate 29. Delores Browne as a member of the New York Negro Ballet Company, circa 1956. Photograph reproduced through the courtesy of the Marion D. Cuyjet Private Collection.

Plate 30. Donna Lowe and Elmer "Skeets" Ball in a ballet class at the Judimar School of Dance, circa 1955. Photograph reproduced through the courtesy of the Marion D. Cuyjet Private Collection.

Plate 31. Judimar School of Dance recital performance of *Giselle*. Donna Lowe bottom center as *Giselle* and Judith Jamison top center as Myrtha, circa 1956. Photograph reproduced through the courtesy of the Marion D. Cuyjet Private Collection.

Plate 32. Judimar School of Dance tap class. On top of piano, L-R Judith Jamison, Tondelaya Simmons, Joyce Graves, Donna Lowe, Sally Richardson, sitting at piano, Edward Riley, standing left at the end of the piano, Prestiss Massey and Stephen Cuyjet Jr. ,right front sitting on floor, Veda Bernardino, circa 1953. Photograph reproduced through the courtesy of the Marion D. Cuyjet Private Collection.

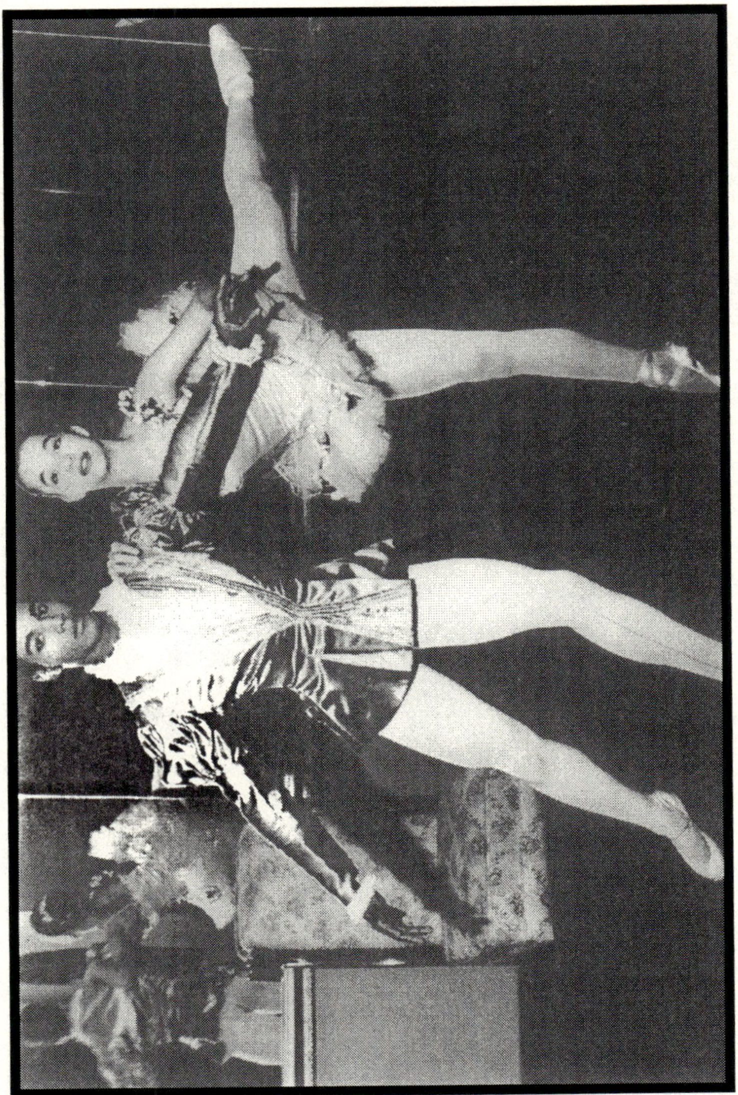

Plate 33. Elmer "Skeets" Ball partners Donna Lowe Warren for a Judimar School of Dance recital, circa 1957. Photograph by E. Barton. Reproduced through courtesy of the Marion D. Cuyjet Private Collection.

Plate 34. Judith (Judy) Marion Cuyjet preparing to perform for the Philadelphia Christmas Cotillion Ball, circa 1960. Photograph reproduced through the courtesy of the Marion D. Cuyjet Private Collection.

Plate 35. Elmer "Skeets" Ball as a member of the Katherine Dunham Dance Company. L-R: unidentified dancer, Katherine Dunham, and Elmer Ball, circa 1959. Photograph reproduced through the courtesy of the Marion D. Cuyjet Private Collection.

Plate 36. Elmer Ball signed this professional portrait: To Miss Marion, with Love Always, "Skeets," circa 1965. Photograph reproduced through the courtesy of the Marion D. Cuyjet Private Collection.

Plate 37. China White, Yvonne Hall, and Brenda Garrett (Glassman) as members of the Theatre of Harlem, circa 1971. Photograph reproduced through the courtesy of the China White Collection.

Plate 38. China White performing in Louis Johnson's *Forces of Rhythm* with the Dance Theatre of Harlem. L-R: China White, Sheila Rohan, Brenda Garrett, unidentified dancer, Yvonne Hall, Stephanie Dabney, circa 1972. Photograph reproduced through the courtesy of the China White Collection.

Plate 39. Marion Cuyjet teaching ballet for Philadanco "company class" at the Philadelphia School of Dance Arts in Philadelphia, Pa., circa 1995. Photograph reproduced through the courtesy of the Marion D. Cuyjet Private Collection.

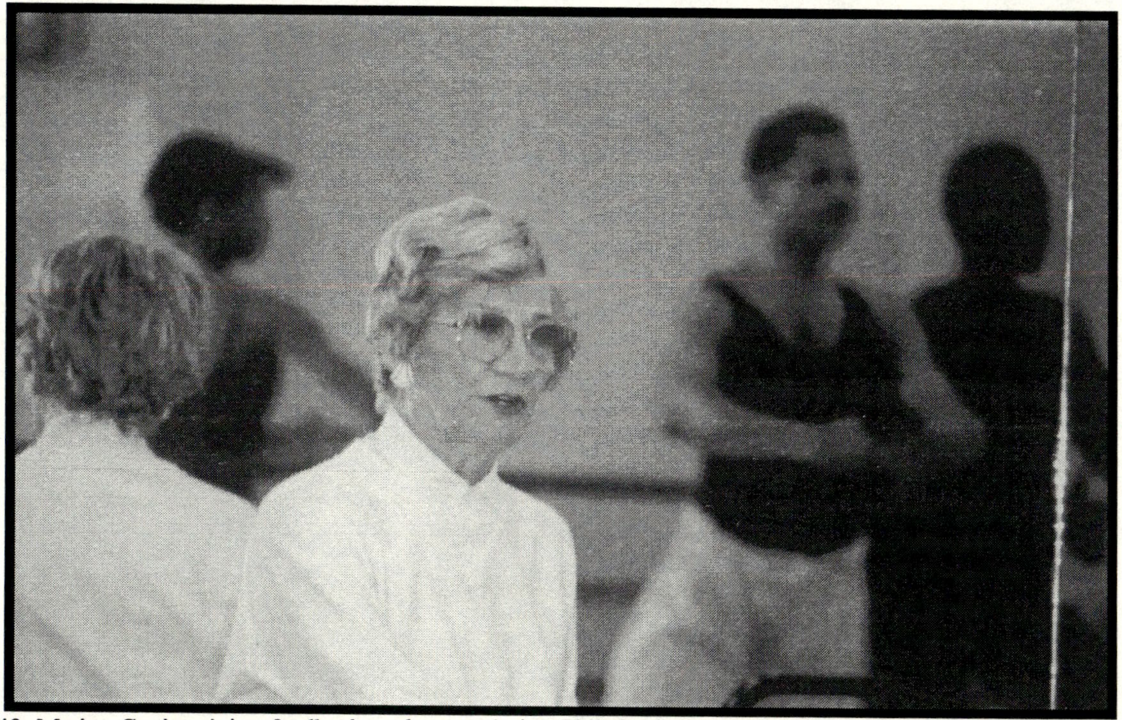

Plate 40. Marion Cuyjet giving feedback to dancers during Philadanco "company class" circa 1995. Photograph reproduced through the courtesy of the Marion D. Cuyjet Private Collection.

References Cited

Abelson, Delores Browne. (1985, August 23). Personal communication-interview. New York City. Melanye White-Dixon.
Ball, Elmer. (1985, September 3). Personal communication-interview. Philadelphia, PA. Melanye White-Dixon.
Ballard, Allen B. (1984). *One more days journey*. New York: McGraw Hill Book Co.
Barham, J. N. & Thomas, W. L. (1969). *Anatomical kinesiology, a programmed text*. London: MacMillan Co.
Black achievements. (1963, January 1). *Philadelphia Tribune*, pp. 23–24.
Blockson, Charles. (1975). *Pennsylvania's Black history*. Philadelphia, PA: Portfolio Publishing Company.
The Blue Venus, ballet hailed as one of finest staged by cotillion. (1955, January 8). *The Afro-American*, p. 15.
Bowser, John. (1981). Minority business and city economic policies. In C. Lewis (Ed.), *State of Black Philadelphia 1981* (pp. 113–120). Philadelphia, PA: Urban League of Philadelphia.
Brown, Joan M. (1977, February 12). Essie Marie Dorsey. *Philadelphia Tribune*, p. 12.
______. (1982, October & 1985, September 20). Personal communication-interview. Philadelphia, PA. Melanye White-Dixon.
Buckle, Richard. (Ed.). (1949). *Katherine Dunham, her dancers, singers, musicians*. London: Ballet Publications, Ltd.
Cazenave, Noel. (1985, January). Black Philadelphia. Class notes. Temple University, Philadelphia, PA.
Celain, Gary D., (n.d.) *Joan Kerr Dance Company*. Unpublished manuscript.
Chujoy, Anatole & Manchester, P. (1967). *The dance encyclopedia*. New York: A. S. Barnes and Company.
Cohen-Stratyner, Barbara. (1982). *Biographical dictionary of dance*. London: Schirmer Books, a division of Collier Macmillan Publishers, 1982.
The colored kiddie hour. (n.d.). Unidentified clipping, Robert Fontell, private collection.
Colvin, Judy Cuyjet. (1985, February 7, September 7). Personal communication-interview. Philadelphia, PA. Melanye White-Dixon.
Cuyjet, Marion D. (1984, November 29; 1985, January 27, July 18, August 13, September 11, 25, October 2, 25; 1986, January 14, April 3). Personal communication-interview. Philadelphia, PA. Melanye White-Dixon.
______. (1970). Resume. M. D. Cuyjet. Private collection
Cuyjet, Stephen, Jr. (1986, March 1). Personal communication-interview. Philadelphia, PA. Melanye White-Dixon.
Cuyjet, Judy. (2010, June 8). Personal Communication-Interview. Mt. Laurel, New Jersey. Melanye White Dixon.

Demille, Agnes. (1963). *The book of dance*. New York: Golden Press.

Dixon, Melanye W. (2004). Judith Jamison. In Gates, Henry Louis & Higginbothem, Evelyn Brooks (Ed.). *African America Lives* (pp. 444–445). New York: Oxford University Press.

Doke, Teri. (1983). The state of Black cultural institutions. In Charyn D. Sutton (Ed.), *The state of Black Philadelphia 1983* (pp. 29–41). Philadelphia, PA: Urban League of Philadelphia.

Dollar, William. (1986, February 16). Personal communication-interview. New York City. Melanye White-Dixon.

Dorsey recital, (n.d.). Unidentified clipping. Essie Marie Dorsey, private collection.

Dra Mu Opera season booklet. (1958–59). Malcolm Poindexter, Sr., private collection.

Drimmer, Melvin (Ed.). (1972). *Black history—a reappraisal.* Garden City, N.J.: Doubleday Publishing Company.

Du Bois, W. E. B. (1899). *The Philadelphia Negro* (1967 ed.). New York: Schocken Books.

Faggins, Barbara. (1985, February 8). Judith Jamison, more than a dancer. *Philadelphia Tribune*, weekend portfolio, pp. 1, 8.

Flyer. (1939, September 9). Announcement of arts symposium series. E. M. Dorsey, private collection.

______ . (1962, September 15). Announcement of Essie Marie Dorsey dance clinic fall session. E. M. Dorsey, private collection.

Fox, Barbara Figge. (1986 April 6). Too-few black companies but two are on their way here. *The Times,* Trenton, N.J. pp. cc6-cc7.

Franklin, Vincent P. (1979). *The education of Black Philadelphia: The social and educational history of a minority community, 1900–1950.* Philadelphia: University of PA. Press.

Gaines, Eddie, (n.d.). Garroway shows Philly's art, talented dancers to the nation. *Philadelphia Afro-American.* Clipping. M. D. Cuyjet, private collection.

Gave vacations to their art. (n.d.). Unidentified clipping. M. D. Cuyjet, private collection.

Giddens, Nancy L. (1986, February 20). Negro history salute to Dr. Eugene W. Jones. *The Philadelphia New Observer*, p. 6.

Goldner, Nancy. (1985, February 9). She has danced far from Phil., but tomorrow is a homecoming. *Philadelphia Inquirer*, pp. 1-D, 3-D.

Gordon, Greer, (n.d.). Cotillion brilliant. Unidentified clipping, reference to E. W. Jones. E. M. Dorsey, private collection.

Grant, Gail. (1982). *Technical manual and dictionary of classical ballet.* (3rd ed.). New York: Dover Publications, Inc.

Greene, Jonnie. (1997, February). classic black-photography exhibit of African American ballet dancers. *Dance Magazine,* pp. 86–91.

Hall, Arthur, (n.d.) Unidentified clipping. Joe Nash collection.

______. (1985, May 22). Personal communication-interview. Philadelphia, PA. Brenda Dixon-Stowell.

Hammond, Sandra N. (1982). *Ballet; beyond the basics.* New York: McGraw-Hill Companies.

Haywood, Claire & Jones, Doris. (1963, March 1). Letter to Marion Cuyjet. M. D. Cuyjet, private collection.

Hershberg, Theodore. (1981). *Blacks in Philadelphia 1850–1980, immigrants, opportunities and racism. In C. lewis (Ed.), State of Black Philadelphia* (pp. 14–22). Philadelphia, PA: Urban League of Philadelphia.

Hines, John. (1984, February 27, 1985, July 24). Personal communication-interview. Philadelphia, PA. Melanye White-Dixon.

Holmes, Percy. (1985, November 12). Personal communication-interview. Philadelphia, PA. Melanye White-Dixon.

Horwitz, D.L. (2003). The New York Negro ballet in Great Britain. In T. DeFrantz (Ed.). *Dancing many drums* (pp.317–338) Madison Wisconsin: University of Wisconsin Press, 2003.

Interracial dance school notes record enrollment, (n.d.). Unidentified clipping. M. D. Cuyjet, private collection.

Jackson, Harriet. (1966, September). American dancer-Negro: accepted in the mainstream. *Dance Magazine*, pp. 19–42.

Jamison, Judith. (1985, February 10). Lecture/demonstration. Philadelphia Museum of Art. Philadelphia, PA.

______. (1993). *Dancing spirit: an autobiography.* New York: Doubleday.

______. (1985, May 16). Personal communication-interview. Philadelphia, PA. Melanye White-Dixon.

John-Hall, Annette. (2009, October 9). At 90, dance master still enpointe. *The Philadelphia Inquirer*, n.p.

Judimar school endorses course in primitive for youngsters. (n.d.). Unidentified clipping. M. D. Cuyjet, private collection.

Judimar school recital bulletin. (1950, 1954, 1955, 1962, 1966, 1970). Philadelphia, PA. M. D. Cuyjet, private collection.

Judimar 1215 Walnut, offers male scholarships. (1951, September 1). *Philadelphia Tribune*, n.p.

King, Sidney G. (1982, November, 1985, February 14). Personal communication-interview. Philadelphia, PA. Melanye White-Dixon.

Kourlas, Gia. (2007, May 6). Where are all the black swans? *The New York Times*, p. 1 section 2.

Kraines, Minda & Kan, Esther. (1983). *Jump into Jazz, a primer for the beginning jazz dance student.* Palo Alto, California: Mayfield Pub. Co.

Kraus, Richard. (1969). *History of the dance in art and education.* Englewood Cliffs, N. J.: Prentice-Hall, Inc.

Long, Richard & Nash, Joe. (1989). *The black tradition in American dance.* New York: Rizzoli.

Mathis, Thadeus P. (1981). The status and growth of Black political independence in Philadelphia 1979–1980. In C. Lewis (Ed.), *State of Black Philadelphia* (pp. 62–64). Philadelphia, PA: Urban League of Philadelphia.

Maynard, Olga. (1982). *Judith Jamison, aspects of a dancer.* New York: Doubleday & Co., Inc.

Mazo, Joseph. (1977). *Prime Movers, the makers of modern dance in America. Princeton, NJ: Princeton Book Co.*

Mondesire, J. Whyatt. (1984). *Facts on Black Philadelphia.* Philadelphia, PA: Author.

Nash, Ione. (1985, September 27). Personal communication-interview. Philadelphia, PA. Melanye White-Dixon.

Nash, Joseph. (1985, August 16). Personal communication-interview. New York City. Melanye White-Dixon.

Obituary program. (1967, June 8). Essie Marie Dorsey. E. M. Dorsey, private collection.

Packman, Jeri. (1986, February 18). Personal communication-interview. Philadelphia, PA. Melanye White-Dixon.

Philadelphia school of dance arts bulletin. (1985, May). Philadelphia PA. J. M. Brown, private collection.

Primus, Pearl. (1985, April 17). Lecture/slide presentation. Department of African American Studies, Temple University. Philadelphia, PA.

Program booklet, Philadelphia cotillion society ball. (1977, December 30). Philadelphia, PA. Vera Gunn, private collection.

Ridley, Harrison. (1985, October 17). Person communication-interview. Philadelphia, PA. Melanye White-Dixon.

Roberts, Doris. (2010, February 15). Personal communication-interview. Columbus, Ohio, Melanye White Dixon

Saunders, John. (1966). *100 years after emancipation, history of the Philadelphia Negro, 1787 to 1963*. Philadelphia, PA: E. R. S. Pub. Co.

Schaunensee, Max de. (1948, May 9). Fine performances feature Dra Mu Opera festival. *Philadelphia Bulletin*, n.p.

______. (1950, October 28). City premiere of Haitian opera given here by Dra Mu singers. *Philadelphia Bulletin*, n.p.

Sims, Patsy, (n.d.). Marion Cuyjet couldn't dance so she produced Judith Jamison. *Philadelphia Inquirer*, Clipping. M. D. Cuyjet, private collection.

Smith, William. (1985, October 14). Personal communication-interview. Philadelphia, PA. Melanye White-Dixon.

Southern, Eilene. (1971). *The music of Black Americans*. New York: W. W. Norton Co.

Stephens, Eazell. (1982, October 7). Personal communication-interview. Philadelphia, PA. Melanye White-Dixon.

Stephens school of dance recital bulletin. (1973, August 26). Philadelphia, PA. E. Stephens, private collection.

Stripling, Alexis Wilson. (2010, February 25). Personal communication-interview. Columbus, OH. Melanye White Dixon.

Sydney school of dance 36th annual recital bulletin. (1983, June 11). Philadelphia, PA. M. W. Dixon, private collection.

Tierney, John. (1975, August 24). It's America's only Black opera company. *Philadelphia Bulletin*, p. AA5.

The unusual interracial dance school, (n.d.). Unidentified clipping. M. D. Cuyjet, private collection.

Vaganova, Agrippina. (1969). *Basic principles of classical ballet* (3rd ed.). New York: Dover Publications.

Wanamaker Junior High School local history club. (1985). *The Edwin Forrest house, an historical landmark.* Unpublished manuscript, John Wanamaker Junior High School, Philadelphia, PA.

Warren, Donna L. (1985, September 28). Personal communication-interview. Philadelphia, PA. Melanye White-Dixon.

Webster, Daniel. (1969, July). Philadelphia company finds its feet. *Dance Magazine*, p. 64.

Weslager, C. A. (1943). *Delaware's Forgotten Folk.* Philadelphia: University of Pennsylvania Press.

White, Clark. (1985, November 22). Personal communication-interview. Philadelphia, PA. Melanye White-Dixon.

White-Dixon, Melanye. (1984, April 30). *John Hines: master teacher of Dunham technique.* Paper presented at Temple University, Dept. of Dance, Philadelphia, PA.

White-Dixon. (1991). The legacy of Black Philadelphia's dance institutions and the educators who built the tradition. *Dance Research Journal of CORD* (23/1). 25–29.

White-Dixon. (1995). Black women in concert dance, the Philadelphia divas. In K. Vaz (Ed.), *Black women in America* (pp. 298–322). Thousand Oaks, California: Sage Publications, Inc.

Wilson, G. L. (1974). *A dictionary of ballet* (3rd. ed.). New York: Theatre Art Books.

Win scholarships to school, (n.d.). Unidentified clipping. M. D. Cuyjet, private collection.

Yancey & Erickson. (1979). Antecedents of community: The economic and institutional structure of urban neighborhoods. *American Sociological Review, (5), 253–262.*

Index

Melanye White Dixon

Dr. Melanye White Dixon is an Associate Professor in the Department of Dance and the Department of African American and African Studies at The Ohio State University in Columbus, Ohio. Dr. Dixon received her Ed.D. in Dance Education from Temple University in Philadelphia, Pennsylvania, where she has been honored as a Temple University Alumni Fellow.